Alpine Club Guide Books

MONT BLANC RANGE I

General Editor: W.H.O'Connor

ALPINE CLUB GUIDE BOOKS

Mont Blanc Range
VOLUME I

TRÉLATÊTE - MONT BLANC
MAUDIT - TACUL - BRENVA

compiled and edited by

ROBIN G. COLLOMB

W.H.O'CONNOR

Alpine Club London

MONT BLANC RANGE Volume I

First published in Britain 1976 by
The Alpine Club London

Copyright © Alpine Club 1976

SBN 900523 20 4

Designed, produced and sold for the Alpine Club by
West Col Productions Goring Reading Berks. RG8 OAP

Produced from manual information storage and retrieval systems
converted to punched tape serial 47A, May 1976

Original diagrams by R.B. Evans modified by
West Col Productions
New diagrams produced from
Frischer-Roberts Archives and West Col Archives

Mont Blanc Range in three volumes consisting of –

Set Olivetti Editor 5C typescript by Rosalind Stayne at
West Col Productions
Printed offset in England by Swindon Press Ltd, Swindon, Wilts.

Contents

Illustrations

INTERNATIONAL ALPINE DISTRESS SIGNAL

A more elaborate system of signals has been devised in Britain but the International system is basic to the subject of attracting attention in an emergency.

Use a whistle, torch or flashes of the sun on a mirror. Alternatively, shout, or wave bright clothing:

Six regular flashes/notes in a minute, repeated at intervals of a minute.

The reply is three signals per minute.

SELECTED BIBLIOGRAPHY

* publications in print or easily obtainable during 1976

Ball, J. Peaks, Passes and Glaciers (First Series). 1859
- The Alpine Guide: Western Alps. Coolidge ed. 1898
* Blodig, K. & Dumler, H. Die Viertausender der Alpen. 1972 ed.
Bonatti, W. On the Heights. 1964
* - The Great Days. 1974
* Bonington, C. J. S. I Chose to Climb. 1966
* Brown, J. The Hard Years. 1967
Brown, T. Graham. Brenva. 1944
- & de Beer, Sir G. The First Ascent of Mont Blanc. 1957
Clark, R. W. The Early Alpine Guides. 1949
- The Victorian Mountaineers. 1953
- An Eccentric in the Alps. 1959
* Collomb, R. G. Chamonix-Mont Blanc. 1969
* Conway, W. M. The Alps from End to End. 1895
Coolidge, W. A. B. The Alps in Nature and History. 1908
Cunningham, C. D. & Abney, W. de W. The Pioneers of the Alps. 1887
Dent, C. T. Above the Snow Line. 1887
* Field & Spencer. Peaks, Passes and Glaciers (Third Series). 1932
Frison-Roche, R. & Tairraz, P. Mont Blanc and the Seven Valleys. 1961
Gervasutti, G. Gervasutti's Climbs. 1957
Gos, C. Alpine Tragedy. 1948
Kennedy, E. S. Peaks, Passes and Glaciers (Second Series). 2 vols. 1862

de Lépiney, J. & T. Climbs on Mont Blanc. 1930

Lunn, A. A Century of Mountaineering. 1957

Magnone, G. The West Face. 1955

Mathews, C. E. The Annals of Mont Blanc. 1898

Milner, C. D. Mont Blanc and the Aiguilles. 1955

Moore, A. W. The Alps in 1864. 2 vols. Blackwell ed. 1939

* Mummery, A. F. My Climbs in the Alps and Caucasus.
        Blackwell ed. 1946

* Pause, W. Im Schweren Fels. 1960

* - & Winkler, J. Im Extremen Fels. 1970

* Rébuffat, G. Starlight and Storm. 1956

-            On Snow and Rock. 1963

-            Between Heaven and Earth. 1965

* -   The Mont Blanc Massif. 1975

Roch, A. On Rock and Ice. 1947

-        Climbs of My Youth. 1949

* Roberts, E. B. High Level Route. 1973

* Scott, D. K. Big Wall Climbing. 1974

* Smith, A. The Story of Mont Blanc. 1853, 1974 ed.

Smythe, F. S. Climbs and Ski Runs. 1929

-            Mountaineering Holiday. 1940

* Stephen, L. The Playground of Europe. Blackwell ed. 1936

* Terray, L. Conquistadors of the Useless. 1963

* Vanis, E. Im Steilen Eis. 1964

* Whymper, E. Scrambles Amongst the Alps in the Years
        1860-69. 6th ed. 1936

* -   Chamonix and the Range of Mont Blanc.
        1896, 1974 ed.

* Young, G. W. On High Hills. 5th ed. 1947

* Technical Climbing Guide Books

Guide Vallot. Ed. Devies, L. & Henry, P.

La Chaîne du Mont Blanc Vol I. 3rd ed. 1973
-                        Vol II. 3rd ed. n.p.
-                        Vol III. 3rd ed. 1975

10

Guida dei Monti d'Italia. Ed. G. Buscaini, R. Chabod,
L. Grivel, S. Saglio

Monte Bianco Vol I. 1963
-           Vol II. 1968

ABBREVIATIONS

AC	Alpine Club
Aig.	Aiguille
Biv.	Bivouac (hut)
c.	approximately
CAAI	Italian Universities Alpine Club
CAF	French Alpine Club
CAI	Italian Alpine Club
Fr.	French
h.	hour(s)
IGM	Italian military map
IGN	French ordnance map
It.	Italian
KF	Kümmerly & Frey (map)
KK	Kompasskarte (map)
km.	kilometre(s)
L	left (direction)
LK	Swiss federal map
m.	metre(s)
min.	minute(s)
Mt.	Mont
mtn.	mountain
P.	Pointe, Punta, Picco (summit)
pt.	point (spot height)
Pte.	Pointe (summit)
R	right (direction)
TCI	Italian Touring Club (map)
UIAA	International Union of Alpine Associations
VT	Vallot map

25m., 50m.   1:25,000 and 1:50,000 map scales
Compass directions are indicated as: N,S,E,NE,SW, etc.

Introduction

PREFATORY NOTE TO 1967 EDITION

The range of Mont Blanc is the most important in the Alps. A new guidebook in English is not only long overdue, it must now be approached with a comprehensive eye for a wider coverage of the range. Most of the routes, of every standard, worth climbing in the range have been included, with the result that the guidebook is published in two volumes. The selection, as such, evolves from eliminating uninteresting climbs and minor variations, but also from an attempt to estimate which climbs will be popular with British parties in the future. This latter point applies particularly to modern routes, where there may be several similar, equally fine and difficult routes on the same face. In addition to the wider selection of climbs, peaks and cols which are not crossed by routes included are mentioned briefly, so that a stranger to the area may acquire a more complete picture of the range.

A high percentage of the descriptions are original compositions, based either on the personal knowledge of the authors or on published accounts of others and information supplied by correspondents. A feature of this treatment is that some descriptions are quite different from long accepted directions for climbing well-known routes; new ways of doing these routes have been established and are reported for the first time. No emphasis has been placed on the traditional British preference for rock climbs. The routes described are what they happen to be - rock, snow, ice or mixed terrain - according to location in the range.

Mountaineering literature, experience and opinions relating to the Mont Blanc region are so extensive and diverse that it is felt unnecessary to dwell at length on the merits of this magnificent range. As a centre for mountaineering the range is the most densely "populated" in the world. In another sense it is also the most competitive without being too specialised in one type of climbing or another. The highest technical achievements are demonstrated here, while the novice can learn the craft in equally perfect situations. The quality of climbing is consistently high and the scenery something more than grand.

There are more accidents and rescue operations in the region than anywhere else in the Alps. The hurly-burly pace of mountaineering at Chamonix and Courmayeur should not be allowed to distract the visitor from the dangers inherent in the pastime. It is because one finds here the finest concentration imaginable of every type of climbing that particular care and circumspection must be exercised to enjoy the mountains to the full.

PREFATORY NOTE TO 1977 EDITION

The original edition of this work (see above) went out of print some years ago and several endeavours to revise and update it failed. Vol. I was reprinted twice to ensure that information about Mt. Blanc in particular remained available for the climbing public, even though some of this information had become long outdated.

In presenting a new edition three volumes have been devised to cover the range, which correspond to the divisions of the Guide Vallot. The treatment within these divisions is however different, while the guide continues as a selection of routes and does not pretend to be comprehensive.

Compared with the previous edition, the content in Vol. I has been enlarged approximately forty per cent. This consists mainly of post-1965 routes and also the addition of some older routes. A considerable amount of alteration has been made to routes described in the previous guide, to account for errors and better descriptions, and in some cases because of changed circumstances for approaching climbs. Historical and first ascent information has been greatly expanded, and skiing activities where they seem appropriate have been recorded.

The grading of routes presents fresh problems as one generation follows another. A majority of opinion has opted for revising grades, usually but not always downwards, and wants to reconcile descriptive general gradings, which previously were applied blanket-wise over all types of climbing, with modern practice. In particular, rock climbs devoid of notable snow/ice difficulties either on the approach or on the route itself are now felt do not warrant an adjectival grading. Only the numerical grade is applied. Against this it must be said that many rock routes involve mixed climbing or snow/ice work in the course of descents by another route, and these can sometimes be serious and might warrant an adjectival grading as high as AD+. The present writer has gone back on some of this, and in a majority of cases has retained an adjectival grading on routes which are predominantly or appear wholly to be rock climbing where such climbing occurs above c. 3750m. At this altitude or higher snow/ice must form an element in a greater or lesser degree, according to conditions and recent weather.

Greatly changed maps since the last guide was issued have complicated writing the new and make scores of new references to mtn. features necessary. Not the least of these problems is the diminuition of spots heights compared with the old Vallot map references, and the introduction of Italian ones from maps not generally available.

It is important to appreciate that the ground covered in this new Vol. I is less compared with the former. The latter included the Chamonix Aiguilles which are now part of the new Vol. II. The areas described in the three new volumes are as follows:

I.   Trélatête - Mt. Blanc - Maudit - Tacul - Brenva
II.   Aiguilles - Rochefort - Jorasses - Leschaux
III. Triolet - Verte/Drus - Argentière - Chardonnet - Trient

In common with introductory remarks in the new Pennine Alps guide (Alpine Club, 1975), mountaineering is now such an expensive pastime that no purpose is served by giving an indication of costs, or advice in detail on how to travel to Chamonix and Courmayeur. At the present time access is easy throughout the year by road or rail. The quickest way remains flying to Geneva international airport from where road/rail connections can be made with a journey of $2\frac{1}{2}$ h. to Chamonix. The motorway (toll) between Geneva and Chamonix is now complete.

Similar comments about huts apply. Reciprocal rights on charges continue to exist between various Alpine countries. In French and Italian huts the scheme has been extended to include members of the Alpine Club. These AC rights do not at present apply in Swiss huts at the NE end of the range. On some cableway and mtn. railway services a reduction is given to holders of a French Alpine Club card, but there is generally no reciprocal rights for others.

Robin G. Collomb
Goring on Thames, September 1976

MAPS

The guide is designed for use with the new official French (IGN) map drawn on a scale of 25m. issued in two sheets covering the entire range, and first published in April, 1973.

(A pilot for this map was issued in 1970 as one sheet in 20m. covering the central part of the range. In retrospect, IGN changed horses in mid-stream and had made an expensive blunder). It was reprinted with a few changes in 1975. This map is a "one-off" special tourist production and does not fit into the IGN grid series of maps. Information on it is generally more up to date, and the presentation of mtn. features is more detailed and drawn in a better way, than its counterpart on the same scale in the grid series. However, many spot heights have disappeared from the new map while some new ones have appeared. The latter are mainly on the Italian side of the range and have come from Italian (IGM) mapping. Heights do not always agree between the new map and the grid map. The grid map has some affinity in its detail with the original Vallot map of the range (in 20m. and 50m., many sheets). The latter contains many more measured heights of secondary summits and spot heights than any subsequent IGN map.

Traditionally the Guide Vallot has always used the Vallot (VT) map for all altitude references. While this map was in general circulation few problems arose. Nowadays it is hard to come by and more than half the sheets in its 20m. grid are out of print. Therefore in this guide Vallot heights are quoted only where they may be of assistance in route finding or assessing a vertical interval between two points. They are indicated as such (VT), and do not appear on IGN mapping.

For the Italian side of the range heights on Italian ordnance maps (IGM) which differ from IGN ones are often quoted in descriptions where the information is considered of value to the climber. Ten years ago these differences were far more numerous but IGN has now adopted a large number of Italian measurements.

For the Swiss end of the range heights on the Swiss federal maps (LK) usually correspond with IGN or IGM, or both as the case may be. The Swiss map is excellent and in its 50m.

grid series covers a large part of the range. In the newer 25m. grid series the mapping does not extend so far along the range, and the previously announced map, sheet 1364, in this scale which would have covered Mt. Blanc itself is not to be published. To simplify compilation of the guide the only reference made to LK maps is on the rare occasion that important conflicting information is revealed. Otherwise the LK maps, so far as they extend along the range, are as good if not better than IGN, and are very much better than any Italian mapping published to date.

The best map in one sheet for gaining a good appreciation of the range at a glance is the Didier & Richard version of IGN 50m. This consists of parts of several grid maps printed together with additional overprinted information, anotations and indexes. A small drawback is that the quality/clarity in printing is not of the same standard as the individual IGN grid sheets.

The original IGN 20m. grid sheets (two) covering the middle part of the range were withdrawn in 1973 and reissued almost immediately in a photographic reduction as 25m. This remains a good quality map but now cannot be used so conveniently with the two additional maps at the St. Gervais end of the range, which used to fit up with the two for the middle part, but remain in the 20m. scale.

There are at least half a dozen other maps generally in 50m. scale produced by commercial concerns. Most of them cover the range rather tightly (too tight, for instance, to show the Tour du Mont Blanc) and are not up to the mapping standard of IGN and LK. On the other hand they are much cheaper. The TCI map has a few references which do not appear on any other map, and these are sometimes quoted in the guide. The most commonly available commercial maps in Britain are listed below with the official IGN and LK maps.

IGN 25m. Massif du Mont Blanc. Carte touristique (2 sheets)

    20m. grid sheets St. Gervais-les-Bains 4
                       St. Gervais-les-Bains 8
    25m. grid sheets Chamonix 5-6
                       Mont Blanc 1-2
    50m. grid sheets St. Gervais-les-Bains XXXV-31
                       Chamonix XXXVI-30
                       Mont Blanc XXXVI-31

LK 25m. grid sheets Col de Balme 1344
                       Orsières 1345
                       Gd. St. Bernard 1365
    50m. grid sheets Martigny 282
                       Courmayeur 292
    50m. district series. Mont Blanc-Grand Combin 5003

Other maps (all 50m.):

DR/IGN Mont Blanc & Beaufortain (recommended)

TCI Gruppo del Monte Bianco D61

KF Mont Blanc-Kette 0721

KK Massiccio del Monte Bianco 85

ALTITUDES AND NOMENCLATURE

Nearly all altitudes are taken from the IGN 25m. special map. Heights which do not appear on this map, or conflict with it, and which are considered important to note are identified from their source, viz. VT, IGM, LK or TCI. Other heights quoted in the guide are approximate calculations from contour lines.

Heights given in graded climbs are the vertical distance from the base of a route (or a designated pt.) to its summit (not necessarily the summit of a parent mtn.), and always exclude the height gained in approaching the climb, say from a hut. A vertical distance is nearly always less than actual climbing distance.

Place names are taken from the IGN 25m. special map. Italian names are sometimes different, and these are given in preamble descriptions.

ORIENTATION

The directions left (L) and right (R) in the sense of direction of movement of the climber - ascent, descent, traverse of slope - have been used consistently throughout. For mtn. features such as glaciers, couloirs, rivers, etc. the traditional orographical reference to left and right banks as viewed in the direction of flow, i.e. downward, has been abandoned, due to the number of complaints received over the confusion this system causes. These features are therefore now described in the sense of movement of the climber. For example, you go up the L side of a glacier, which was previously described as ascending the R bank. In some descriptions both ways are given to emphasise orientation. Compass directions are also given to assist route finding.

WINTER AND SKI ASCENTS

Following decades of disagreement on the validity of winter ascents according to dates recorded, a recent UIAA recommendation that the period for counting winter ascents should run from 21 December to 20 March has met with disfavour in some quarters. Doubtless general adoption of this period would eliminate many claims to notable first winter ascents made up to 15 April, sometimes later. Without wishing to enter into the argument, in this guide dates from 21 December to 31 March are admitted as winter ascents. The guide also reports important ascents on ski at any time of the year. The contemporary "sport" of "extreme ski", being the descent of snow and ice faces on ski, is recorded for appropriate routes.

CAMPING

A number of authorised campsites with good toilet and washing facilities are to be found in the Chamonix valley. The largest are at Les Pèlerins and Les Chosalets (Argentière).

There are many smaller ones, some closer to Chamonix, with variable and sometimes poor facilities. There is no approved public campsite in the near vicinity of Courmayeur. Private camping can be arranged in advance with certain landowners on the outskirts of the village; consult with tourist office. The main public sites are some distance from Courmayeur. A very large one, more like a holiday camp with limited shopping facilities, is found in Val Veni a short distance above the Cantine de la Visaille (made up roadhead and bus terminus); another in the Val Ferret above Montita. There was no evidence of authorised camping at Entrèves in 1974. Visitors without cars may find these campsites very inconvenient. Camping at Courmayeur is generally disapproved of and is kept as far away from the village as possible.

GRADING OF CLIMBS

In accordance with the UIAA classification system, the grading of rock climbs is numerical from I to VI and A1, A2, A3 and A4 for artificial. Grade I is the easiest and VI the hardest. Variations of difficulty are denoted by + and - signs; plus is above the normal rating and minus below (i.e. V-/V/V+). These variations above grade IV will matter for the expert climber and should be equally helpful in the lower grades for the average performer. It must be stressed that the grade of a climb is determined not only by pure technical difficulty but also by objective danger and length.

Mixed climbs and snow/ice climbs are also graded in six stages. This grading is always more approximate and less precise than the numerical rock grades because of variable conditions in a season and from year to year. Winter climbing will be different again, and apart from severe cold grades could be lower or higher according to the nature of the route. In order of rising difficulty: F (easy), PD (moderately difficult),

AD (fairly difficult), D (difficult), TD (very difficult), ED (extremely difficult). Further refinement is possible by adding plus or minus signs.

MOUNTAINEERING TERMS, LANGUAGE AND CURRENCY

For the most part terms used in this guide, though not always proper English words, will be known and understood by alpinists. A glossary is considered unnecessary. In Chamonix and Courmayeur relatively little English is spoken. French is widely understood on the Italian side of the range. Good currency exchange facilities exist in both resorts, at banks, hotels, stations and tourist offices. The rate of exchange for presenting the wrong currency at huts is unfavourable, e. g. Italian lire in a French hut.

Valley bases

VAL MONTJOIE

This valley flanks the range at a tangent, running N to S at the western edge of the region. The entrance at the N end is Le Fayet. There is a good train and bus service from Chamonix to Le Fayet in 45 min.

St. Gervais-les-Bains. Frequent bus service from Le Fayet in 10 min., or the Mont Blanc Tramway can be taken. From St. Gervais the tramway climbs above the Val Montjoie, reaching the Col de Voza, Bellevue and Nid d'Aigle (terminus). See Chamonix valley below for the shortest route from Chamonix to join the tramway at Bellevue. St. Gervais is a comfortable holiday resort, more picturesque than Chamonix and certainly quieter. All classes of hotels, shops, public services, etc.

Les Contamines. In the upper part of the valley, served by buses from Le Fayet and St. Gervais several times a day in summer. Get off at the Miage bridge for the Miage chalets and Durier hut. Hotels and shops at Les Contamines. CAF chalet at Les Contamines in location marked on IGN 25m. map. Buses do not normally go to the roadhead at Notre-Dame de la Gorge. Campsite and parking 2 km. from roadhead.

CHAMONIX VALLEY

Described as far as it is applicable to Vol. I of the guide. Above Le Fayet the main valley makes a big loop N then S before running SW-NE alongside the range.

Les Houches. At the bottom of the second loop and the first village in the valley proper. The village is scattered over a wide area. The station in the valley bottom is one km. from hotels and shops along the slip road above and to the S of the main road. From Chamonix (20 min.) it is better to take a bus going directly into the village. From the railway station go back up the main road towards Chamonix. After crossing the river take the first turning on the R and go up to the slip road leading back to the village. About $1\frac{1}{2}$ km. along this road is the Bellevue cableway station. Cable cars depart every 10 min., terminus on the Mont Lachet ridge (Bellevue, 1794m.) beside the Mont Blanc Tramway (halt).

Les Bossons. Small village 4 km. outside Chamonix. No interest to climbers. Simond's equipment factory is here.

Chamonix. On main line and road between Le Fayet and Franco-Swiss frontier (ultimately Martigny). All classes of shops, hotels, services, etc. CAF office at bottom of road leading to main station. The Montenvers railway lies across a bridge just beyond the main station. The Midi cableway is 10 min. walk from town centre out on the Pélerins road. Cable car service in two stages, to the Plan de l'Aiguille and Aig. du Midi (very expensive). The terminus connects across the range with the Italian Géant cableway. The first stage runs every 10 min., the second every 30 min., weather permitting.

On the W side of the town there is a cableway service in two stages to the Brévent and, higher up the valley, to la Flégère and the Index, starting from les Praz. Excellent views of the Mont Blanc range opposite, and plenty of short rock climbs on the Aigs. Rouges summits behind the cableway termini.

There is cheap bunkhouse accommodation at the Montenvers (rack railway terminus).

The Mont Blanc Tunnel road, from Chamonix to Courmayeur, enters the mountainside above Les Pélerins. This is a toll road, not cheap but nevertheless cheaper than the cableway and much quicker. There is a bus service through the tunnel. Passports are necessary.

COURMAYEUR AND VAL VENI

Courmayeur is quickly reached from Chamonix through the Mont Blanc road tunnel. From Italy there is a bus from the railhead at Pré St. Didier and the journey takes a few min. The tunnel road bypasses the village and has a slip road leading into a large carpark and the centre. All classes of hotels, shops, etc. A bus service runs to the Cantine de la Visaille in Val Veni; the road beyond that is very rough. There is another service to Entrèves at the entrance to Val Ferret; here is the lower station of the Géant cableway with frequent departures in two stages to the Torino hut and Col du Géant, expensive. Continuation service in two stages to the Midi station above Chamonix.

Huts and other mountain bases

FRANCE

Trélatête Hotel 1970m.

Hôtellerie de Trélatête.   Privately owned.   Situated on a shoulder above the terminal tongue of the Trélatête glacier. Simple hotel service, open all summer and much of the winter. Room for 80. Telephone.

1 From Les Contamines in Val Montjoie, go by road to the Cognon hamlet and then by mule track via Les Plans sur Cognon (1534m.) to the hotel (2½ h.). Or from Les Contamines take the road to Notre-Dame de la Gorge and then a track via the Combe Noire (3 h.).

Conscrits Hut 2730m.

Refuge-bivouac Conscrits.   CAF property, situated on the true R bank of the Trélatête glacier and on a small moraine platform below the S ridge of the Bérangère. The hut is rough and without a warden but has bedding and some cooking equipment to cope with 14 persons.

2 From the Trélatête hotel (Route 1) follow the footpath that makes a rising traverse E, taking a L fork at a branch, to the moraines alongside the glacier tongue. In the most northerly corner a shelf slopes down to the glacier (45 min.). Ascend the glacier close to rocks on your L, turning open crevasses on the L. At the foot of the first icefall, below the Tréla-grande (large rockbanks), it is usual to ascend the steep ice slope near its centre, crampons useful; in certain conditions a better route can be forced near the L edge (45 min.). Above the icefall go along the glacier about 300m. from the Tréla-grande bank, turning long open crevasses on the L. The glacier gradually bends L (NE). Having just turned the corner at c. 2550m. move L on to a moraine strip not far below a more crevassed section of the glacier directly adjoining the Conscrits hut and ascend loose stones above the glacier to the hut (45 min., 2¼ h. from Trélatête hotel). Helicopter landing pad on a terrace somewhat higher.

Durier Hut 3349m. VT

Refuge Durier. Property of the CAF. Situated on the Col de Miage, somewhat below the ridge crest on Fr. side, and at the top of a central rock buttress rising from the Fr. Miage glacier. The Col de Miage (q. v.) is an undulating crest with the lowest pt. at the S end (3342m.). The hut is near the N end, adjoining trig. pt. 3358m. This small hut has been improved recently, no warden, room for 8-10, water source just below hut platform.

3   From Tresse (1016m., dormitory chalet) on the St. Gervais-Contamines road in Val Montjoie follow the lane to the last houses near the Miage stream, then take the large track winding S to the Maison Neuve pasture (1290m.), continuing to climb generally E in a traverse through forest to reach the Miage chalets (1559m.) (1¾ h.). Continue on a small track near the centre of the alluvial flats ahead, keeping to the L side of the main stream. At the end of this section climb a rock barrier near pt. 1710m. and just R of a waterfall. Now ascend moraine and a slabby rock barrier, keeping L, into a narrow valley below and S of pt. 2092m. (falling ice possible). Go up this and move on to the grassy lateral moraine to your R. Follow its crest till a traverse R can be made to the main glacier at c. 2550m. (Plan Glacier on map). Traces of a path all the way (2¼ h.). On the other side of the glacier is a big broken rock buttress with low relief ribs and shallow couloirs under the Col de Miage, base pt. 2760m.

According to conditions on the glacier, reach the buttress either by crossing the glacier SE under a crevassed steepness in the slope, or keep L and climb above and round this steepness (small séracs) before crossing the glacier to reach the

28

buttress at a slightly higher pt. Cross a bergschrund then ascend the main central rock rib, getting steeper and looser with big unstable blocks towards the top, where the hut is found. This pt. is L of the lowest pt. of the col. In good snow conditions the couloir on the R of the central rib can be quicker, while in similar conditions that on the L can be climbed or descended equally well. Traces of a track on the rib itself. In a dry season the bergschrund should be crossed well to the L in ascent ($2\frac{1}{2}$ h., about $6\frac{1}{2}$ h. from Tresse). PD.

4   Courmayeur side. Start from the entrance to the large campsite complex on the alluvial flats of the Lac de Combal. Leave the road in Val Veni at the first bridge over the river and take a rougher road and path NW, under the large lateral moraine enclosing the Lac du Miage. By this path (which bears L) cross over the moraine by a track to the R and get on to the It. Miage glacier. Follow the stone covered glacier more or less in its centre, with open crevasses higher up. Below the Aigs. Grises it becomes snow covered and more care should be taken with crevasses ($2\frac{1}{2}$ h.). Continue up the L side of the glacier to the foot of the fairly steep snow slope near pt. 2925m. under the Col de Miage ($1\frac{1}{2}$ h.). Now climb easy rock steps and snow on the L, towards a small snow cap (3390m.) somewhat L of the main ridge saddle. Just short of this summit, slant R up to the ridge and follow the crest in a few paces over the regular crossing pt. 3367m. and trig. pt. 3358m. to the hut a few m. below and 30m. away ($1\frac{1}{2}$ h., about $5\frac{1}{2}$ h. from bridge near Combal lake flats). PD.

5   From the Trélatête hotel (Route 1). The shortest way is to follow Route 30 to Col Infranchissable (3349m.), then take Route 31 to pt. 3672m. of the Dômes de Miage. From this snow summit resist the temptation to wander off L and descend its NE ridge as described in Route 31a by a fine narrow snow crest. On reaching the Col de Miage, after an initial saddle (3342m.) follow the snow ridge with a few rocks beyond (3390m.) to a second saddle (3367m.), the true col, and a characteristic rock thumb (3358m.). The hut is located on the Fr. side of the crest, some 30m. distance from the rock thumb (about 7¼ h. from Trélatête hotel). PD/PD+.

Tête Rousse Hut   3167m.

Refuge de Tête Rousse. Property of the CAF. Situated near the foot of the cliffs of the Aig. du Goûter, on the true L bank of the small Tête Rousse glacier (helicopter landing pad). Warden and simple restaurant service in summer. Telephone.

6   From the Chamonix valley it is best to take the cableway from Les Houches to Bellevue (1790m.). From here one can take the Mt. Blanc tramway to the Nid d'Aigle terminus (2372m.). A good track leads from Bellevue to the same point (beware of branches leading off to the Bionnassay valley). From the terminus, the path continues S for 200m., then turns L (avoid branches to R) and zigzags up below a rocky escarpment into a debris filled hollow, just S of the main ridge known as Les Rognes. After reaching a small hunters' cabin (2768m.) the path turns sharp R (SE) to mount the ridge of the Aig. du Goûter which here is mainly scree and broken rocks, but sometimes covered with snow. Zigzag up this ridge on a good path, then traverse right across the Tête Rousse glacier to the hut opposite (2½-3 h. from Bellevue).

7   From the Montjoie valley one can either take the Mt. Blanc tram way all the way from Le Fayet-St. Gervais, or good paths from St. Gervais and Bionnay lead to Bellevue and thence to Nid d'Aigle. Then as for Route 6.

Goûter Hut   3817m.

Refuge de l'Aig. du Goûter. Property of the CAF. Situated on a ledge on the W side of the Aig. du Goûter (3863m.), just below and N of the summit snow cap. The highest fully equipped hut in the Mt. Blanc range; the new building was completed in 1962. It has room for 76, provides hotel service, warden resident in summer. Visitors are not allowed to cook their own food. Goods transporter lift from Tête Rousse hut not normally available for rucksacks. Telephone.

8   From the Tête Rousse hut go up the R side of the Tête Rousse glacier to a low and broad depression in the long rib which descends from near the summit of the Goûter, and which divides the Tête Rousse and Bionnassay glaciers. From here one can follow any of the ribs directly above or a little L over steep unpleasant rocks to the top of the cliffs and the hut (PD-). The big couloir on the R can be seldom used because of serious stonefall.   Some parties climb it in the hours of darkness but this is not recommended.   The rib to the R of the couloir is the easiest and normal way, but crossing the couloir is exposed to stonefall and late in the season it is often bare ice. A fixed cable has been put across the couloir and safety bays have been cut beside rock outcrops in the slope. Great care should be exercised when crossing this place. On the other side a broad broken rib of steep loose rock is climbed in short zigzags (traces of path) directly to the hut at the top (2-3 h. from Tête Rousse hut). F+.

Vallot Hut   4362m.

Refuge Vallot - Mt. Blanc. Property of the CAF. Situated near the foot of the Bosses ridge, close to the line of the normal route up the mtn., and on a prominent rock outcrop called the Foudroyés. A duralumin shelter with room for 24. Re-equipped in 1968 but it is often in a squalid state. The hut should only be used in an emergency.

Grands Mulets Hut   3051m.

Refuge des Grands Mulets. Property of the CAF. Situated on the Grands Mulets rocks above the junction of the Bossons and Taconnaz glaciers. A classic site on which a succession of buildings has been erected. Completely rebuilt in 1960, with 70 sleeping places, hotel service and resident warden in summer. At the moment apparently more popular with spring skiers. Telephone.

Visitors to this hut have been decreasing to such an extent in the 1970s that publicity campaigns have been run to popularise it to combat talk in some quarters of closing it down. The route up Mt. Blanc from this hut is just as fine and as worthwhile as that from the Goûter hut, while their respective routes join at the Col du Dôme.

9 From the Plan de l'Aiguille cableway station (2310m.) go up the well marked path towards the Pèlerins glacier. Traverse the glacier almost horizontally to the W at c. 2375m. below the Aig. du Midi. Continue traversing by a good path to the derelict cableway station of the Gare des Glaciers (2414m.). From here the path traverses to the Bossons glacier under the large couloir of the Aig. du Midi (stonefall). Reach the glacier, go up its L side for a short way then cross it SW (Plan Glacier) towards the slightly higher and very crevassed area of la Jonction. Work up to below then R of the Grands Mulets rocks (very crevassed, plank bridges placed across particularly wide chasms). Ascend ruptured snow slopes on this R side of the rocky island, and finally move L to a path with an iron handrail going up to the hut (3 h. from cableway). The traditional walking routes from the valley have been ignored in favour of this much shorter approach from Plan de l'Aiguille now used by nearly all visitors to the hut.

Col du Midi Hut   3600m.

Abri Simond. Privately owned. Situated at the foot of the SW ridge of the Aig. du Midi, about 700m. N of the col proper (3532m.). Originally built for the construction of the cableway, disused and in a poor state of repair until its recent revival. Simple meals from a warden, places for 10 to 12. Reached from the Midi cableway station in 20 min. or so by descending on steep snow at first, round below the E and S faces of the Aig. du Midi. Patronised by skiers.

Midi Cableway Station   3795m.

On the N summit of the Aig. du Midi. A convenient starting point for many expeditions. Tunnel and gallery leading to the NE ridge for access to the Vallée Blanche. Officially climbers are not allowed to stay there, but in emergencies the cableway staff allow one to sleep on spare mattresses for which a small charge is usually made.

ITALY

Elisabetta Soldini Hut   c. 2280m.

Rifugio Elisabetta Soldini-Montanaro. Owned by the CAI. Situated just above the lower chalets of Lex Blanche (2258m.), at the end of the rough motor road in Val Veni. The road is unmade and poor after la Visaille (1659m., bus terminus). A modern hut with room for 45, restaurant service, warden resident in summer.

10 From Courmayeur take the road up Val Veni. There is a good surface (but much of it under repair in 1974) as far as la Visaille, bus service, 2 h. walking. Continue up the road past the extensive campsite complex on your R (Combal) and so to the lower Lex Blanche chalets (2 h., 4 h. from Courmayeur on foot, accessible by car).

Estelette Bivouac   2958m.

Bivacco Adolfo Hess. Owned by the CAAI. Situated just above the Col d'Estelette (2924m.), well seen from the Elisabetta hut. A small bivouac with room for 4, generally not in a good condition. A new hut is proposed.

11 From the Elisabetta hut follow the path which goes to the R (N) of the Pyramides Calcaires. Ignore two L forks and after the second turn R and cross below the tongue of the Estelette glacier. Climb up the R (N) side (traces of path) to the broad scree fan coming down from the col. Go up this to a steep loose couloir rising to the gap, sometimes with snow in the bed, and follow it to the top. From here climb a loose broken rock ridge W, track in places, keeping L, for 50m. distance. Then cross the ridge crest line to the R (N) side where the hut is found a few m. below the crest (2½ h. from Elisabetta hut). F.

Petit Mt. Blanc Bivouac 3047m.

Bivacco Giovane Montagna. Owned by the Giovane Montagna group and built in 1963. Situated on rocks immediately below the snowy section of the SE ridge of Petit Mt. Blanc (3424m.), and overlooking the Aigs. de Combal (2839m.). Room for 8, door open, take your own stove, etc. The best starting point on the Courmayeur side for normal routes on the Trélatête summits.

12 In Val Veni, at the bridge L over the river and at the entrance to the campsite complex near the Combal flats, turn R and follow a bad road to a parking place under the big moraine concealing the Lac du Miage. Down to the L a path continues in the same direction (NW) along the edge of the flats to the moraine abutting the rock barrier-grass terrace flank of Mt. Suc. This path (not marked on any map) now climbs diagonally L (W) across the flank, along grassy ledges and rakes rising through easy rock bands, and enters a narrow cwm-valley coming down between the Aigs. de Combal (L) and Mt. Suc (R) above. The path continues its traverse line; ignore this. Turn up the narrow valley and ascend it with an intermittent track improving higher up, over grass and rocks in the bed. After passing between the two guardian marker summits on either side, bear L on to the saddle spur behind the Aigs. de Combal. From here make a rising traverse L to avoid some rocks on the spur, then go up directly over rocks and snow patches to the hut in a conspicuous position (3 h. from bridge in Val Veni). F.

Gonella (Dôme) Hut 3071m.

Rifugio Francesco Gonella. Owned by the CAI. Situated above

the true R bank of the Dôme glacier, on the spur descending SE from the ridge of the Aigs. Grises. A new hut with room for 50, warden resident in summer.

13 From the bridge over the river near the Combal flats in Val Veni follow Route 4 up the lt. Miage glacier till you are opposite the foot of the Aigs. Grises ridge about pt. 2523m. Cross the glacier R and leave it some 150m. L of pt. 2523m. where a path is found at the entrance to a scree couloir. This path rises steeply R in rocks and grass then goes up more rocks and across a shoulder on to the Dôme glacier side of the Grises ridge. Continue the rising traverse, more to the N, dropping a little before crossing snowfields and moving R across couloirs and up on to the rocky spur where the hut is situated overlooking the glacier ($4\frac{1}{2}$ h. from bridge in Val Veni). F.

<u>Quintino Sella Hut</u>   3396m. IGN   3371m. TCI

Rifugio Quintino Sella. Owned by the CAI. Situated on the SW slopes of the Rocher du Mont Blanc, the complex spur dividing the Dôme and Mont Blanc glaciers. No warden, room for 15, door open. Water from the glacier.

14 From the bridge over the river near the Combal flats in Val Veni follow Route 4 up the lt. Miage glacier to the junction on your R with the Mt. Blanc glacier. Climb the L-hand (N) branch of the glacier close to the buttress of the Rocher spur (N of the rognon 2980m. and often very crevassed), and move L to reach the buttress by the first grassy couloir at c.2600m. If the crevasses or the bergschrund prevent access to the couloir, an oblique chimney on the L side of the couloir may give an easier alternative. Leave the couloir at one third height, slanting R up steep grassy slopes on a faintly marked track. A rock wall and a poorly defined couloir lead almost directly to the crest of the Rocher ridge. Follow the ridge, keeping mostly to the R (E) side. Pass an old hut at c. 3100m. and turn the last rocks on the R up a scree/snow couloir to reach the hut which is not seen till the last moment $(6\frac{1}{2}$ h. from bridge in Val Veni). F+.

<u>Gonella (Dôme) - Quintino Sella huts connection</u>

A useful connection, slightly exposed to stonefall in the couloir. F+.

15 From the Gonella hut descend a small track to the Dôme glacier and cross it to the foot (3003m. on IGN 20m. map) of a large Y-shaped couloir some 400m. high which descends from the SW spur of the Rocher du Mont Blanc. Climb the couloir, keeping to the rocks on its R side (least exposed to stonefall) in the lower section, then take the R-hand branch to reach the crest of the spur near the Quintino Sella hut. Avoid climbing the centre of the couloir $(2\frac{1}{2}$ h.).

<u>Monzino Hut</u>   2590m.

Rifugio Franco Monzino. Owned by the Courmayeur Guides' Association. Situated on a spur between the tips of the Brouillard and Frêney glaciers, above and to the N of the Aig. du Châtelet. The hut is slightly lower than the old Gamba hut, which has now been destroyed. A superb modern hut with sleeping places for at least 50. Warden in summer, simple hotel service. Special room and dormitory for visitors wishing to cook their own meals. The hut also has a winter room with 6 places. Service cablelift from near la Visaille which can be used to send up rucksacks to the hut.

16 From the Chalet du Miage on the main road in Val Veni, cross the Doire and follow the path to the Frêney chalets (1589m.). From here a signposted path to the L is taken up through woods to cross the Frêney glacier torrent and reach the foot of steep slopes on the E side of the Aig. du Châtelet. The main path continues L (W) towards the Miage glacier. Leave this and zigzag up these slopes to the R on a well marked path, to reach a steep barrier of slabs in three tiers with fixed cables. Marker posts, etc. Above the barrier the path continues and reaches the crest of the spur behind and N of

the Aig. du Châtelet. The hut is a few min. higher, overlooking the Frêney side (2½ h. from road).

Eccles Bivouac c. 3850m.

Bivacco Giuseppe Lampugnani. Owned by the CAAI. Not
precisely marked on any map. Situated about 200m. below
the summit of Pic Eccles (4041m.) on its SW ridge. The foot
of this short ridge in the Brouillard glacier is pt. 3759m.
IGM. A tiny bivouac shelter protected by an overhanging
block. Room for 6, blankets. A long tiring approach with
variable route finding mainly on snow and some ice. PD.

17 From the Monzino hut follow the track in rocks and moraine
to the N up to the tiny Châtelet glacier. The best line is to
follow a faintly marked path which goes diagonally up the L
side of the moraine. Climb near the R side of the glacier and
ascend a short barrier of smooth wet rocks to reach easy
scree slopes on the S side of the Innominata. Trending L,
climb scree and broken rocks to the S ridge of the Innominata
at a shoulder (3281m.) below the foot of its first gendarme.
On the other side a short diagonal descent leads to the Brouillard glacier.

Early in the morning, and in good snow conditions, it is
quicker to follow the R side of the Brouillard glacier from
the moraine above the Monzino hut. This joins the route on
the W side of the S ridge of the Innominata.

Go up the badly crevassed glacier, passing the foot of a
rock buttress (3376m.) coming down from the summit ridge
of the Innominata. Cross a bergschrund up to its L and go
diagonally on a low line up steep snow slopes to the far N end
of the Col de Frêney saddle (3680m.). This col is between
the Innominata and Pic Eccles (4-5 h.). From the col climb
a steep snow/ice slope to a small snow terrace. From here
continue L up snow then mixed ground with loose rock to the
biv. hut which can be seen from afar and is visible from a

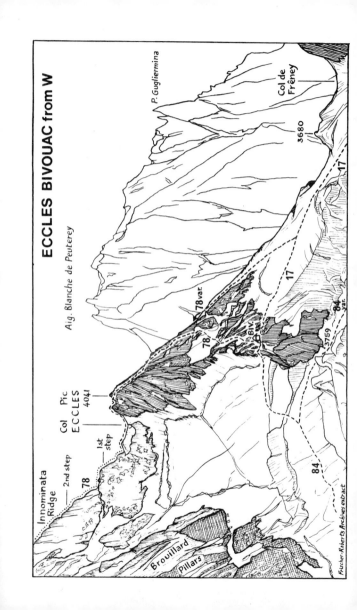

ECCLES BIVOUAC from W

Innominata Ridge
2nd step
78
1st step
Col Pic
ECCLES 4041
78var.
78
61v.
P. Gugliermina
Aig. Blanche de Peuterey
3680
Col de Frêney
17
17
3759
84
84 var.
84
Brouillard Pillars

Fischer-Roberts Archives extract

long way down the Brouillard glacier (1-2 h., 5-7 h. from Monzino hut).

Dames Anglaises Bivouac 3490m.

Bivacco Piero Craveri. Owned by the CAAI. Situated on the Brèche Nord des Dames Anglaises, slightly on the Brenva side. Room for 5. A long tedious approach with frequent stonefall in the Dames Anglaises couloir. AD/AD+.

18 From the Monzino hut climb grass and moraine (track) to the N up to the tiny Châtelet glacier. Go up the R side of this first over a zone of smooth slabs and continue up snow to the base of the narrow couloir leading to the Col de l'Innominata (3205m.), which is just N of the Aig. Croux. Rotten rocks in the couloir lead to the gap L of a small gendarme ($2\frac{1}{2}$ h.). On the other side descend steep rotten rocks, going R then L (abseil) to avoid a steep step, in all 75m. down to the Frêney glacier (30 min. - 1 h.). Now cross the very crevassed glacier slightly upwards to the bergschrund below the couloir of 300m. coming down from the Brèche N des Dames Anglaises (1 h.).

Cross the bergschrund on the L, often quite tricky, and climb the couloir on snow or ice or use rotten rocks on its L side, to the junction with the couloir dropping from the Brèche Centrale. Bad stonefall possible to this point. Continue climbing the L branch, very narrow and enclosed between impressively smooth walls, till it is possible to transfer to broken rock on the L side just below the gap. From here descend a few m. half L to the biv. hut ($1\frac{1}{2}$-3 h., $5\frac{1}{2}$-$7\frac{1}{2}$ h. from Monzino hut). Many parties have successfully done this approach at night and in comparative safety using powerful head torches, in about 4 h. Crossing the Frêney glacier is the trickiest part in darkness on account of route finding through the crevasses.

<u>Noire Hut</u>   2316m.

Rifugio Lorenzo Borelli, renamed Pivano. Owned by the CAAI. Situated in the Fauteuil des Allemands cwm, on the R side under the rocks of the Mt. Noir de Peuterey. A new hut was built in 1969 on the site of the previous hut. Room for 35, no warden, fully equipped, door open. Water from a nearby stream. The approach involves a bit of rock climbing, PD with short pitches of II, III.

19 From Le Purtud in Val Veni, follow the path on the R side of the Doire through a campsite and past the Peuterey chalets (1501m.). Leave the main path before it crosses the stream issuing from the Fauteuil, and follow a poorly marked path across this stream at a higher level. By a small and steep zigzag track in scrub-covered scree climb the cone which splays out from the rock barrier guarding the Fauteuil. At the top of the scree cone traverse R and slant up to a rock rib. Climb a short steep pitch of red rock (II), then zigzag up ledges to a smooth pale-coloured slab, close to the L side of the main stream. Climb the slab (5m., III) and cross the stream. Ascend rightwards in the direction of an isolated clump of trees and cross a second stream; then return L before reaching the trees and climb a slab with cut holds (II) before recrossing the second stream. Now go more or less straight up between the streams, trending first L then up a short chimney (III) followed by a large slab (II) taken on its L side. Continue up the grassy rib near the main stream; the angle eases into the cwm; cross the stream R and follow the path keeping R to the hut (2½ h. from Le Purtud).

<u>Brenva Bivouac</u>   3140m.

Bivacco della Brenva. Owned by the CAAI. Situated about halfway up the rognon which descends SSE from the Col de la Tour Ronde, alongside the true L bank of the main Brenva glacier. Position wrongly marked on IGN, which is c. 150m. too far W. The exact location is just below the 0 in spot height 3140 on map. Room for 4, door open, water nearby. A useful alternative starting point for the Brenva face routes. F+.

20 From Entrèves above Courmayeur spoil tips below the entrance to the Mt. Blanc tunnel have erased the start of the path. The best way is to cross the motorway approach near pt. 1310m. by an underpass and take the lorry road under the tips to the W. This leads to the Brenva chalets (1517m. IGM). In the same direction (W) a small valley is formed between the Brenva moraine and the wooded mountainside. Take a small track, the upper of two, along the R side of the valley to a rock barrier at its top which extends L-wards to the Brenva moraine. Climb the barrier by a short scree couloir, exiting R up grass, then contour L round the base of the Rochers de la Brenva. Continue up grassy slopes and soon cross a small stream to an old moraine which is followed NW to the upper extremity of rocks in this direction, under the SW side of the Aig. de la Brenva.

Cross the glacier at a narrow flattish section NW to a wedge-shaped inlet in the broad base of the large rocky rognon above. This is R of its lowest pt. and just L of pt. 2807m. This is the entrance to a couloir splitting the R side of the rognon. Climb the couloir on scree and loose blocks, higher up keeping to its R side, and after 100m. exit R up a break line rising due N to the hut which is near the edge of a glacier branch further R (about $5\frac{1}{2}$ h. from Entrèves).

<u>Col de la Fourche Bivouac</u>   3680m.

Bivacco Alberico e Borgna. Owned by the CAAI. Situated slightly on the It. side of the Col de la Fourche de la Brenva (3682m.), somewhat to the SE at the foot of the NW tower of the Fourche (3737m.). Room for 8-10. The N (usual) approach involves steep snow/ice climbing, AD+.

21 From the Requin hut follow Route 27 as far as the Bédière plateau. Cross this plateau and continue more or less straight up the glacier under the Gross Rognon. Somewhere in this region the track usually divides. A L-hand one goes to the Torino hut, the R-hand to the Col du Gros Rognon for the Aig.

du Midi. Continue straight up the glacier (SSW), under Pte. Adolphe Rey and the Capucin, into the Maudit-Tacul glacier bay. Normally you have to swing well to the L to avoid large crevasses. Aim straight for the Col de la Fourche, cross the bergschrund below it and climb the steep snow/ice slope or rocks on the right in a shallow couloir line (neither is easy) to the col. Move a few m. along a fine snow crest to the L and descend a few rocks to the biv. hut (4-5 h. from Requin hut).

22 From the Midi cableway station descend steep snow to below the S face of the Midi. Traverse across the head of the Vallée Blanche (usually tracks) to the Col du Gros Rognon (3415m.). Descend slightly under the NE face of Mt. Blanc du Tacul and contour round the base of the Pyramide du Tacul and Pte. Adolphe Rey, where Route 21 is joined ($3\frac{1}{2}$ h. to biv. hut).

23 From the Torino hut follow the tracks below Pte. Helbronner and the Grand Flambeau, and cross the shoulder of the Col des Flambeaux (3407m.). Make a descending traverse round the huge glacier bay, finally climbing under the N face of the Tour Ronde to reach the N slope of the Col de la Fourche, where the previous routes are joined at the bergschrund (Torino hut - Fourche biv., $3\frac{1}{2}$ h.).

24 From the Brenva biv. hut ascend diagonally L over blocks and scree to a short rock wall which is climbed direct to the top of the rock section of the Brenva rognon, where its continuation snow spur commences. Follow this fairly steep spur, narrowing higher up, to a snow cap under and due S of the Cols de la Tour Ronde. Now traverse a narrow glacier plateau to the W, crevasses in same direction, until the main upper plateau of the Brenva glacier is reached, under the

Trident col and peak on the frontier ridge above. Continue up the plateau to below the Col de la Fourche. Cross a bergschrund and climb a snow/ice slope in a couloir and some rotten rocks on its L side to the col and biv. hut, PD+ ($2\frac{1}{2}$-3 h. from Brenva biv.).

Trident Hut   3690m.

Rifugio Lucia e Piero Ghiglione. Property of the CAI. A prefabricated duralumin hut built in 1967, situated on the Brenva side of the Col du Trident (3679m.) and about 50m. distance SE from the col. Small dining/cooking room, sleeps 30, no warden, door open, snow water. A more convenient base than the Fourche biv. for routes on the Brenva face, for example, but not for the frontier ridge of Mt. Maudit.

25 From the Requin, Midi and Torino departure points the approaches correspond with Routes 21, 22, 23. To the L of the Col de la Fourche is the obvious Trident de la Brenva pinnacle. Climb the snow cone below the rocks of the NW spur of the Trident, then cross the bergschrund, usually by an avalanche cone on the R. Above this fixed ropes are in place all the way down the R-hand side of the spur. These lead up broken rocks to the col. Move L across snow to the hut on a rock platform a little higher (4 h. from Requin hut, 3 h. from Midi cableway, $2\frac{1}{2}$-3 h. from Torino hut). PD+.

26 From the Brenva biv., as for Route 24, till on the upper Brenva glacier plateau you are below the snow/ice couloir rising to the Col du Trident. Cross a large bergschrund generally with ease by moving well L, then work up the L side of the couloir, normally straightforward in crampons, to the col ($2\frac{1}{2}$ h.). PD.

Torino Hut   3322m. IGM, old hut
3371m. (3375m. IGM), new hut

Rifugio Torino, adjoining the Col du Géant (3365m.). The lower building, situated at the cableway station, is owned by the CAI. Room for 66, warden and restaurant service in summer and for a lot of the winter and spring. A few min. walk above this hut is the privately run 'grand hotel' of post-second world war origin, complete with television, dance floor and lounge-bar; restaurant service, places for 110 in rooms and dormitories. Open for most of the year. The Col du Géant can be reached from Chamonix and Courmayeur by the trans-range cableway system.

27 From the Requin hut follow the track leading horizontally to the Géant glacier. The Géant icefall has to be climbed. The route and difficulty vary from year to year but there are usually tracks. After the first badly crevassed section trend up R towards a rock island known as the Petit Rognon. Just before reaching it turn to the L and traverse on to La Bédière, a large plateau cut by enormous crevasses. Cross the plateau in the direction of the Col du Géant, keeping to the L (E) of La Vierge and the Petit Flambeau. From the col go slightly R to the rocks on which the hotel stands, and descend in a few min. to the CAI hut and cableway station (3 h.). In poor visability all this ground is bad for route finding. F/F+.

28 From the Midi cableway station follow Route 22 across the Col du Gros Rognon and below the foot of the NE face of Mt. Blanc du Tacul. Continue in the same general direction (SE) to join Route 23 below the Tour Ronde. Now reverse Route 23 across the Col des Flambeaux and continue to the Col du Géant (2-3 h.). F.

29 From La Palud above Courmayeur, a steep and unpleasant path winds up the hillside near the cableway pylons to Le Pavillon. From here the path is easy at first, then it follows a loose broken ridge in endless zigzags to a scree/snow field and more rocks leading to the cableway station and CAI hut (4-5 h.). This approach is hardly ever used by pedestrians, but it is descended fairly often, which is ruinous to the path.

Trélatête · Bionnassay · Goûter group

COL INFRANCHISSABLE 3349m.

This pass lies at the head of the Trélatête glacier, between the Tête Carrée (3732m.) and the second highest and most northerly summit (3672m.) of the Dômes de Miage. The Italian side is quite steep and exposed to stonefall, AD, down to the head of the It. Miage glacier; this side is rarely climbed and is not described. First traverse of this pass: J. Eccles with M. C. Payot and M. Bellin, 1870.

The French side is important as an approach from the Trélatête hotel to numerous climbs on the Dômes de Miage and the Trélatête glacier peaks which flank the Trélatête glacier. A long glacier trudge of $8\frac{1}{2}$ km., badly crevassed after end July.

30 From the Trélatête hotel (1970m.) follow Route 2 to the point on the glacier where you can move L towards the Conscrits hut. Instead, continue up the glacier and work through a crevassed zone opposite the hut by generally keeping L. Higher up (2800m.) snow covers the glacier; unless it is hard, a sharp lookout must be kept for concealed crevasses. Continue in the centre of the glacier, broad and monotonous and split by several big crevasses, to the snowy saddle of the col. Aircraft landing markers just below saddle ($4\frac{1}{2}$ h. on average from hotel, half this time from Conscrits hut).

DÔMES DE MIAGE 3673m.

An attractive snow ridge, extending NE-SW and capped by five summits. The ridge proper commences at a R angle in the frontier, where a spur comes down to Col Infranchissable. From here the tops are: 3672m., 3673m., 3633m., 3666m. and 3670m. The saddle between pts. 3673m. and 3633m. is the Col des Dômes (3564m.). The traverse of all summits is a classic expedition and quite easy. The NW face nowadays has a good selection of snow/ice routes mostly in the D class, of which two are described.

First ascent of highest pt.: E. T. Coleman with F. Mollard and J. Jacquemont, 2 September, 1858. First winter ascent: Mme. V. Bally-Leirens with J. and C. Ravanel, January, 1925. On ski: Capt. de Gemmes, L. Feberey, MM. Fleith and Sexauer, 24 May, 1926. Frequently climbed on ski but not advisable after early June because of numerous crevasses.

Traverse of the Main Ridge. This popular excursion is best undertaken from NE to SW, to avoid descending the Trélatête glacier in the afternoon. Highly recommended. F+. First traverse not recorded.

31 From the Trélatête hotel follow Routes 2, 30 to Col Infranchissable ($4\frac{1}{2}$ h.). A short distance below the saddle steer L and climb fairly steep snow; then return R (crevasses) and aim for the rocky frontier ridge which is reached by negotiating a badly crevassed zone. Follow the rock and scree ridge until it gives on to snow, and go up this to a point about 30m. R of Pt. 3672m. (2 h.). Turn L (S) and follow the main ridge easily to Pt. 3673m. (15 min., $6\frac{3}{4}$ h. from hotel).

Descend the main snow ridge W to the Col des Dômes (3564m.), narrow and sometimes corniced (15 min.).

(Many parties join the ridge at the Col des Dômes by ascending the glacier bay below it directly from the Trélatête glacier. The entrance to this bay is split by large crevasses; $4\frac{1}{2}$ h. from hotel to col).

Now follow the pleasant snow ridge in a splendid position; the ridge is sometimes capped by small cornice lips; cross Pts. 3633m. and 3666m. to reach Pt. 3670m. (45 min.). Continue by descending a broader snow ridge then broken rocks to the Col de la Bérangère (3348m.) (30 min.). From this col ascend an abrupt and narrow corniced ridge, finishing on pleasantly steep rocks at the summit of the Aig. de la Bérangère (45 min., 2 h. from Col des Dômes, 9 h. from hotel).

From this summit reverse Route 34 to the hotel ($2\frac{1}{2}$ h.,

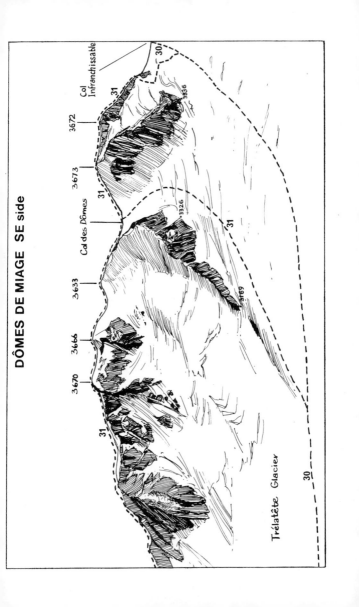

DÔMES DE MIAGE SE side

Col Infranchissable

3672

3673

Cd des Dômes

3633

3666

3670

31

31

31

31

31

31

3336

3326

3169

30

30

Trélatête Glacier

$11\frac{1}{2}$ h. for round trip, or 9 h. by going directly to the Col des Dômes).

31A From the Trélatête hotel the traverse of the main ridge is not infrequently taken in the direction SW-NE, finishing at the Durier hut (3349m. VT) on the Col de Miage. This is a particularly interesting way of doing the expedition, staying at the Durier hut overnight, and in the morning either descending to the valley or continuing the fine traverse over the Aig. de Bionnassay to Mt. Blanc.

In this direction ascend Route 34 to the Aig. de la Bérangère ($4\frac{1}{4}$ h.), and continue by Route 31 along the main ridge to Pt. 3672m. ($2\frac{3}{4}$ h.). From here follow the ridge crest, steep and narrow, down to the Col de Miage (3342m.) (1 h.) which is detailed in Route 5. PD (8 h. from hotel to Durier hut).

North-West Ridge of Pt. 3673 (Voie Mettrier). The best and most popular route on the N side of the Dômes ridge, rarely climbed up to 1960, now recognized as an outstanding route of its class. With good snow early in the season the standard is about PD+. Normally AD/AD+, delicate. 1100m. Conditions vary on the upper part which is steep, exposed and can be very icy. First ascent: Henri Mettrier with F. Carcey and J. Cayetto, 23 August, 1902. First winter ascent: F. and P. Curral, B. Favray, A. Fisseau and M. Morand, 19 January, 1964. Descended on ski by P. Clément and A. Giraud, 22 June, 1968.

32 In Val Montjoie the nearest sleeping quarters (rough) are the Miage chalets (1559m.) on Route 3. Continue by Route 3 to the Plan Glacier of the Miage glacier ($2\frac{1}{4}$ h.). Now traverse R (falling ice) to the opposite S side, below the ridge. Above and R the ridge flank contains a large shallow couloir depression. L of this depression is a fairly steep, rounded rock

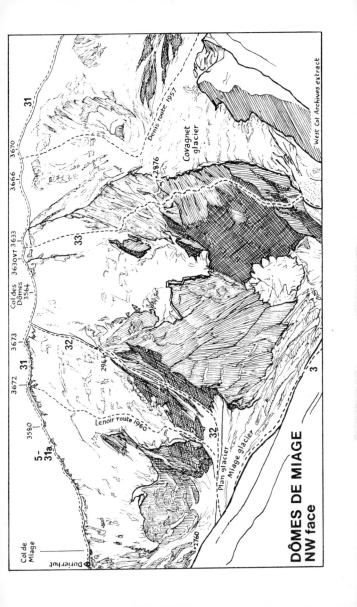

DÔMES DE MIAGE
NW face

West Col Archives extract

Col de Miage

Durier hut

3580

5–
31a

31

3672

32

3673

Col des
Dômes
3564

3630vr 3633

33

3666 3670

31

Denis route 1957

Covagnet glacier

2876

Lenoir route 1960

2946

32

Plan glacier

Miage glacier

Tré-la-Tête
glacier

2760

3

spur, cut by a narrow couloir in its crest line which rises to pt. 2944 on the main ridge above. Either climb the narrow couloir on snow and rock, or rocks further L, to a small saddle in the ridge just below pt. 2944. Continue up the easier rock ridge to the foot of the upper snow section. Keeping slightly R first go up a steep snow/ice slope in two short bulges and return L to the well defined crest line. This steepens progressively towards the top (50°) to exit, possibly through a cornice, on the Dômes ridge approx. midway between Pt. 3673 and the Col des Dômes (6 h., 8¼ h. from Miage chalets).

33 <u>North-West Face of Pt. 3633.</u> The line runs up between two parallel, narrow and short rock ribs descending from the main ridge at Pt. 3633 (R) and a small rock step (L) measured as Pt. 3630 VT in the direction of the Col des Dômes. The R-hand rib is the terminal section of the NW ridge of Pt. 3633 (relatively easy). D, 50-55°, fine ice climbing in a safe situation. First ascent: P.-G. Blanc and P. Dujon, June, 1950. First winter ascent: M. Berruex and P. Curral, 5 January, 1974.

Approach from the Miage chalets by Route 3. At pt. 1710 in the Miage valley bear R (SE) along the lateral moraine abutting the rocks and cliffs on the L (NE) side of the Covagnet glacier tongue. Above the moraine bear L across the flank of the spur coming down from pt. 2876 by a depression (usually snow), followed by a broken rock slope, short steps and ledges rising steeply L to a wide sloping rock terrace above the cliffs bordering a hanging glacier further L. Follow the terrace not far below the crest of the spur until the lowest snow shoulder below the face is reached. Up to the R rises the NW ridge. Traverse diagonally L over steepening snow/ice into the centre of the facet in line between two obvious rock ribs above, then go directly in a fine position to the summit ridge,

50

through a short rock band at the top (7-8 h. from Miage chalets).

AIGUILLE DE LA BÉRANGÈRE 3425m.

The mtn. at the SW end of the Dômes de Miage ridge, frequently combined with a traverse of the latter. Also often done as a training climb from the Trélatête hotel, or from the Conscrits hut. First ascent: Thomas Hare with D. Fournereaux, August, 1858. First winter ascent: Mme. V. Bally-Leirens with J. and C. Ravanel, January, 1925. On ski: MM. L. Feberey, C. Dumoulin, Fleith and Sexauer, 22 May, 1925.

South-West Flank (Trélagrande). The normal route, F. Small track in several places. First ascensionists.

34 From the Trélatête hotel follow Route 2 to the glacier plateau above the first icefall, alongside the broad and easy-angled rocky slope called the Trélagrande ($1\frac{1}{4}$ h.). Reach the L side of the glacier, broken by huge crevasses, and ascend the rocky barrier above in the bed of the second stream to the E (R), which breaks through the barrier. There are traces of a path on its R side. This is roughly midway between pts. 2455 and 2492. Go up this open ravine then cross scree, grass and snow patches beside pt. 2700 to a conspicuous moraine crest ahead. Continue upwards over snow and rocks to the N, passing L of pt. 2931. A steeper snow slope is ascended on the L ($1\frac{3}{4}$ h.). Now aim for the broad snow humps forming the SW ridge of the mtn., and follow them to the terminal rock pile ($1\frac{1}{4}$ h., $4\frac{1}{4}$ h. from Trélatête hotel). Many variations possible over a broad front.

From the Conscrits hut climb a slope of large rocks NW and reach near pt. 2931 the approach from the Trélatête hotel ($2\frac{1}{4}$ h. from hut to summit).

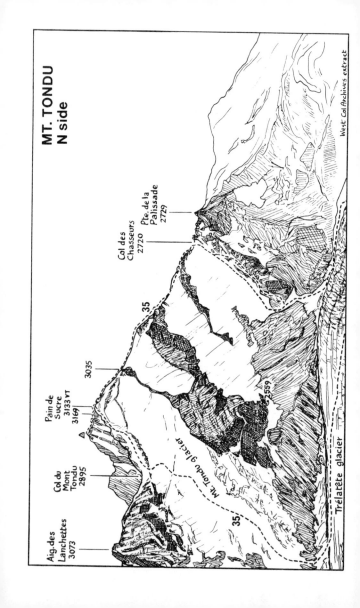

MT. TONDU
N side

West Col Archives extract

Aig. des Lanchettes 3073

Col du Mont Tondu 2895

Pain de Sucre 3133 vt 3169

3035

35

Col des Chasseurs 2720

Pte. de la Palissade 2729

2559

Mt. Tondu glacier

35

Trélatête glacier

MONT TONDU 3196m.

An attractive little peak flanking the S side of the Trélatête glacier in its lower reaches. The snowy N slopes converge at the Pain de Sucre (3133m. VT, not marked on IGN). From this pt. a narrow rock ridge extends to the S, and the highest pt. is near the far end of it. A popular training climb. First recorded ascent: M. Baudry and P. Puiseux, 21 August, 1889. First winter ascent: Mme. V. Bally-Leirens with J. and C. Ravanel, January, 1925.

Traverse by North-West and North-East Ridges. The ascent to the Pain de Sucre is often made by mtn. walkers, although one slope is quite steep and one snow ridge very narrow. The final rock ridge is an interesting scramble, pleasantly exposed. Extensive views to S. F+.

35 From the Trélatête hotel follow Route 2 to the centre foot of the icefall below the Trélagrande. Cross to the R side of the glacier and go up the edge of the icefall into a large open couloir on the R (snow) between two broken buttresses. This lop-sided couloir descends from the Col des Chasseurs (2720m.). Ascend it easily, just below rocks on the R all the way to the top. The R-hand rocks may be scrambled, first by a ledge system on the R, then back to the L into the couloir about two-thirds way to the col (2 h.). Above, a near-vertical rock step in two stages on the NW ridge is climbed directly by a narrow winding track; an abrupt snow/ice slope separates the upper tier from the lower, and the upper one is steepest. A broad snow ridge with some rocks now leads to a cairn at the foot of a narrow rock rib (1 h.). Climb the rib just below the crest on its R side, arriving at a snow ridge whose fine crest (or R flank) runs up nicely to the Pain de Sucre (1 h.). Go along the serrated and almost horizontal rock crest to the S, on excellent rock with plenty of holds. Turn the sharpest teeth on the R by descents of 2-3m. (30 min., $4\frac{1}{2}$ h. from Trélatête hotel).

Return along the rock crest to the Pain de Sucre (30 min.).

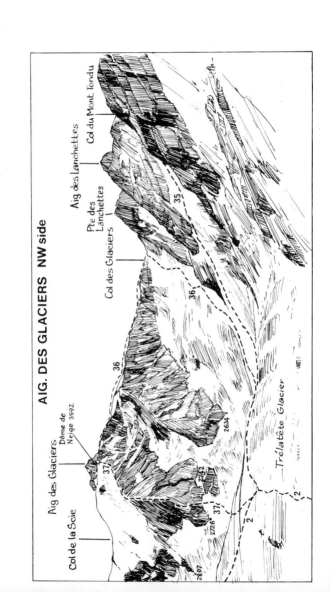

AIG. DES GLACIERS NW side

Col de la Scie

Aig des Glaciers

Dôme de Neige 3592

37

36

Col des Glaciers

Pte des Lanchettes

Aig des Lanchettes

Col du Mont Tondu

35

36

37

2742

2726

2634

2807

2

2

Trélatête Glacier

Descend a slope to the NE, somewhat L of the true ridge crest
and above a parallel bergschrund line. On arriving just below
the Col du Mont Tondu (2895m.), drop down to a few rocks on
the R, then descend the snow slopes of the Mont Tondu glacier
(a few crevasses) running down to the Trélatête glacier. Go
through a short rock barrier on to the glacier and rejoin Route
2 (2 h., 2½ h. from summit, 7 h. for round trip. NE ridge in
ascent, 3¾ h.).

COL DES GLACIERS 3063m.

Between the Pte. des Lanchettes and Dôme de Neige (of the
Aig. des Glaciers). A pass from the Trélatête glacier to the
Lanchettes cwm adjoining the Col de la Seigne. Rarely
crossed. F+. See Route 36. First traverse: W. Mathews
with D. Balleys and Mattex, 24 August, 1866.

AIGUILLE DES GLACIERS 3816m.

A complex mtn. flanking the E side of the Trélatête glacier,
and covered on the S and E (Italian) sides by other glaciers,
which account for the name. The summit ridge is entirely
rocky, formed at the junction of three ridges: N, SE, S (then
SSE). A fourth ridge running from the Col des Glaciers
(3063m.) to the Col de la Scie (3626m.) is generally but in-
correctly called the W ridge; it is important on account of
forming the rim that encloses the Trélatête glacier. This
ridge meets the base of the N ridge above the Col de la Scie
at a large snow hump christened the Dôme de Neige (3592m.).
The mtn. is most easily climbed from the Italian side.
    First ascent: E. Del Carretto and F. Gonella with L. Proment
and G. and A. Henry, 2 August, 1878. On ski: Armand Charlet
and Camille Dévouassoux, 24 May, 1925. First winter ascent:
A. Adami, 14-15 March, 1948.

French (Trélatête) side

West Ridge (from Col des Glaciers). Ridge running WSW from
the Dôme de Neige. The normal Trélatête route, PD/PD+.
Crampons useful. First ascent: A. Archinard, E. Dunand,

C. Fontannaz, F. Geny, S. Miney and C. Montandon, 18 July, 1900.

36 From the Trélatête hotel follow Route 2 to the base of the small glacier below the Col des Glaciers at c. 2500m. (2 h.). From the W (R) corner go up the slope with rocks out-cropping on the R. After a bergschrund-like crevasse cross the head of the rocks up to the R and continue obliquely into the centre of the glacier branch below the col. It is usually best to go across to the R side, before returning to the middle of the now much narrower and steeper slope, so as to pass between two more bergschrunds. Go straight up to the final bergschrund just below the col. It can sometimes be turned on the L beside some rocks. The short final slope is steep and usually icy. The broad saddle of the ridge is adorned by two large rocks (2 h.).

Starting from the Conscrits hut descend S and SW across the Trélatête glacier (crevasses) to the W foot of the small glacier (45 min.).

From the Col des Glaciers follow the ridge, at first rocky, passing a little gap called the Col Moyen Age. The ridge later broadens, becomes stony and runs out into a snow ridge capped by the Dôme de Neige. Shortly before reaching the dome, contour to the R round a snowy cwm at the head of the Glaciers glacier, across a steep snow/ice slope and a few stones. Aim for the base of a rock rib, not very obvious, which descends directly from the summit ($2\frac{1}{4}$ h.). Climb the rib from its lowest point; the rocks are nearly vertical, somewhat loose, but not difficult. Go up the crest to a short snow ridge which leads to the summit (1 h., $7\frac{1}{4}$ h. from Trélatête hotel, 6 h. from Conscrits hut).

<u>North-West Spur of West Ridge</u>. The most direct route from the Trélatête hotel. Steep loose rock for several pitches and a fine snow crest. Practised more than Route 36. AD. First

ascent: J. Lasneret with C. Blanc, 14 August, 1926.

37 From the Trélatête hotel follow Route 2 to the foot of the second rock spur descending from the W ridge, marked pt. 2726 ($2\frac{1}{2}$ h.). From the Conscrits hut cross the glacier directly to the same pt. (20 min.). On the R side of the ridge toe a little snow bay is formed and enclosed by rocks (pt. 2742) further R. Start 30m. up and R from the toe. Climb some steep slabs followed by steep loose rocks leading to the rock crest. Climb the crest to a fairly steep snow ridge and follow this to an abrupt finish at the W ridge not far below the Dôme de Neige. A small cornice may guard the junction (2 h.). Now join Route 36 by traversing R below the Dôme ($1\frac{1}{2}$ h. to summit, 6 h. from Trélatête hotel, 4 h. from Conscrits hut).

Italian side

38 <u>South Ridge (from Estelette glacier).</u> This route (first ascensionists) was reported in the previous edition of the guide as the easiest on the mtn. It is still reported in foreign publications as the shortest and normal route from the Elisabetta hut (about $6\frac{1}{2}$ h.). However all descriptions are suspiciously brief. The Estelette glacier is badly crevassed, sometimes impassible, and above the glacier the couloir-seamed E rock wall under pt. 3607 on the S ridge, which must be climbed, is sometimes scarred by stonefall. One British party reporting on the route since 1967 turned back because of serious stonefall. The technical grade is about PD, but not recommended due to aforesaid remarks.

<u>South Ridge (from Col de la Seigne).</u> This is the simplest route from the Elisabetta hut, and the one followed by most parties. It is quite circuitous and fairly long but in good conditions the ground can be covered quickly. Above the Col de la Seigne (2516m.) the ridge rises in a series of grassy,

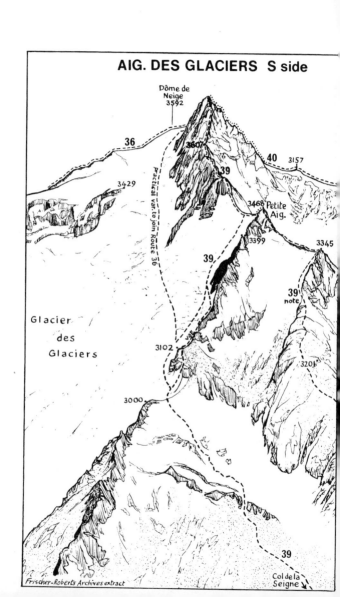

AIG. DES GLACIERS S side

Dôme de
Neige
3592

36

3607

39

40   3157

3429

3468 Petite
Aig.

3399

39

3345

39
note

Practical var. to join Route 36

Glacier

des

Glaciers

3102

3201

3000

39

Col de la
Seigne

Frischer-Roberts Archives extract

schistose-scree and snowy humps, broken in places by low rockbands, up to the Petite Aig. des Glaciers (3468m.). All of this ridge can be climbed at F+, slightly on its L (French) side to the Petite Aig., from where a short descent on rock leads to a snow saddle at the foot of the S ridge proper of the parent mtn. This approach to the latter saddle is normally 30 min. longer than the alternative approach described below. The ridge proper is PD with a pitch of II+/III. A varied and interesting expedition requiring experience due to poor rock. First ascent: M. Baretti with S. Henry, J. J. Maquignaz and A. Sibille, 7 July, 1880.

39 From the Elisabetta hut descend to the jeep track in the valley and go up it towards the Col de la Seigne. Above the last chalets (2285m.) the track bears a little R to cross a stream. After the stream leave the track and ascend grass slopes and scree NW towards the first elevation (2747m.) on the ridge above the Col de la Seigne. Finish up to the R (N) of this elevation on a saddle at c. 2700m. ($1\frac{3}{4}$ h.). Now traverse more or less horizontally L, away from the ridge line, gradually bearing NW over grass and schist to snow patches running up in the direction of a snow saddle ahead, between pts. 3000 and 3102 in the SSW ridge of the Petite Aig. This opening gives access to the Glaciers glacier. Continue up the glacier by its R edge, fairly close to the SSW ridge. There can be a troublesome crevasse zone not far up. In this event an easy alternative is to go up the SSW ridge from the saddle, over pt. 3102, till another saddle is reached, from which you descend a few m. L on to the glacier just above the crevasse zone. Continue keeping close to the ridge up a headslope to a prominent snow saddle at the top, with the Petite Aig. summit just above it to the R ($2\frac{1}{2}$ h.).

Now turn to the main S ridge and climb an initial rock step direct and easily to a narrow crest at the top. Follow the

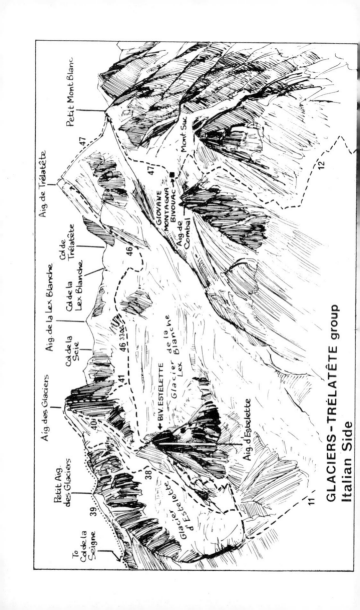

GLACIERS – TRÉLATÊTE group
Italian Side

Petit Mont Blanc

Aig de Trélatête

47

47

GIOVANE
MONTAGNA
BIVOUAC

Mont Suc

Aig de Combal

12

Col de la
Trélatête

Col de la
Lex Blanche

46

Aig de la Lex Blanche

Glacier de la
Lex Blanche

Aig des Glaciers

Col de la
Scie

46 3300

41

← BIV. ESTELETTE

Petit Aig.
des Glaciers

40

38

Glacier
d'Estelette

Aig d'Estelette

39

11

To
Col de la
Seigne

crest, turning difficulties on the R, till a large ledge is reached. Above this climb a steep loose wall with snowbands (pt. 3607), then descend and cross a tricky gap to continue along the ridge to the foot of the final riser. Take steep rocks directly above either by a vague rib or, preferably, by one of the couloirs alongside it. The rocks are unsound and lead to a forepeak. From here cross a narrow snow crest of 30m., normally corniced, to the summit ($3\frac{1}{4}$ - $3\frac{3}{4}$ h., $7\frac{1}{2}$ - 8 h. from Elisabetta hut).

<u>South-East Ridge</u>. The classic route, AD with several delicate pitches of IV and some stonefall danger. First ascent: M. von Kuffner with A. Burgener and J. Furrer, 29 July, 1887 by Var. (i). Direct: L. A. Bergera and I. Brosio, 25 August, 1925.

40 From the Estelette biv. (2958m.) follow the snowy ridge, keeping on the L side. After turning a large gendarme, cross to the R (N) side and traverse steep slabs on good holds, finally traversing small gendarmes to reach a snowy shoulder at the foot of the ridge proper (1 h.). A series of steep steps on fairly sound rock lead up past two gendarmes to a general narrowing of the ridge, now serrated and unsound; this section is liable to be quite delicate in conditions of fresh snow. Higher up the ridge levels out (scree and snow), then rises abruptly in better rock. Climb this, then traverse delicately across the head of a couloir on the L side of the ridge, about 100m. below the summit. A little higher the ridge is blocked by a huge red gendarme, some 60m. high, with an overhanging base (3 h.). Start beside a large rock situated a few m. to the L. Climb a series of walls on small holds (50m., delicate, IV), finishing beside large blocks which lead to the summit (45 min., $4\frac{3}{4}$ h. from Estelette biv.).

Var. (i). It is possible to turn the big gendarme by traversing R, delicate and dangerous, with the aid of a pendulum

61

abseil of 20m. into an ice couloir, which is then climbed by a rock rib on its R side to exit just below the summit.

Var. (ii). The gendarme can also be turned on the L, regaining the ridge by a long and entertaining chimney.

East Face Direct. An excellent rock climb, 500m. D. There is an easier and less satisfactory route to the L, and a new route made in 1974 to the R, which is also easier and by all accounts just as good. First ascent: G. Boccalatte, P. Ghiglione and M. Piolti, 4 September, 1933.

41 From the Estelette biv. (2958m.) follow Route 40 to the snowy shoulder at the foot of the SE ridge proper (1 h.). Descend across a snow slope R to the Lex Blanche glacier and ascend below the NE-E face of the mtn. to the·base directly below the summit (45 min.). Climb an ice slope (stonefall); on the upper part traverse the slope to the L for about 40m. to reach a prominent little couloir. Climb the steep icy couloir to a large ice bulge; exit to the L, difficult and delicate. Now ascend to the R, climbing an easy central rock pillar. Higher up the rocks become progressively smoother and more difficult. Climb them slightly to the R. Several interesting pitches across smooth slabs lead to below a cave. Keeping to the R, climb an exposed ridge, followed by a horizontal ridge. A pleasant climb on the upper part of the face finishes on the N ridge about 5 min. from the summit (4½ h., 6 h. from Estelette biv.).

AIGUILLE DE LA LEX BLANCHE   3697m.

A secondary summit on the ridge between the Aig. des Glaciers and the Aig. de Trélatête. It affords fine snow/ice climbing but is seldom visited. First ascent: V. Attinger and L. Kurz with J.-B. Croz and J. Simond, 25 July, 1889.

<u>North Ridge.</u>   The shortest and easiest approach from the Trélatête hotel side, and the quickest descent. PD, delicate. First ascensionists.

42 The ridge is reached beyond (further N than) the Col de la Lex Blanche (3555m.), at or near Pt. 3569. This is also the access point to the ridge for the normal French route on the Aig. de Trélatête.   Follow the latter Route 44 to below Pt. 3569, then slant R on to the ridge near the slight depression of the Col de la Lex Blanche (6 h., or $3\frac{3}{4}$ h. from Conscrits hut).   Continue on the ridge to the summit over rocks then a very narrow corniced crest (1 h., 7 h. from Trélatête hotel, or $4\frac{3}{4}$ h. from Conscrits hut).

<u>North-West Face.</u> A variable glacier face giving good practice for more serious climbing.   Near the top normally easier exits can be made R on to the W ridge, from below the sérac bulge, or L on to the N ridge, above the sérac bulge. The parallel W ridge is a climb of much the same standard. AD/AD+. First ascent: R. Gaché, P. Gayet-Tancrède and R. Jonquière, 31 July, 1931. First winter ascent: M. Bozon, C. Mattal, F. and G. Mollard, 16 January, 1971. Descended on ski by J. Bessat, 1974.

43 From the Trélatête hotel follow Routes 2, 30 till just passed the Conscrits hut, then cross the glacier to the opening at the foot of the face (pt. 2908 to L) ($2\frac{3}{4}$ h.). About 50m. distance L of the W ridge rock promontory, climb straight up a snow slope over multiple bergschrunds to a narrowing, which is taken L of a small rockband and associated outcrops. Continue up a plain snow/ice slope with increasing steepness on the R side of a sérac bulge. Persevere direct, cross a terminal bergschrund and finish up a very steep slope to the summit (about $5\frac{1}{2}$ h., $8\frac{1}{4}$ h. from Trélatête hotel, 6 h. from Conscrits hut).

Trélatête glacier basin

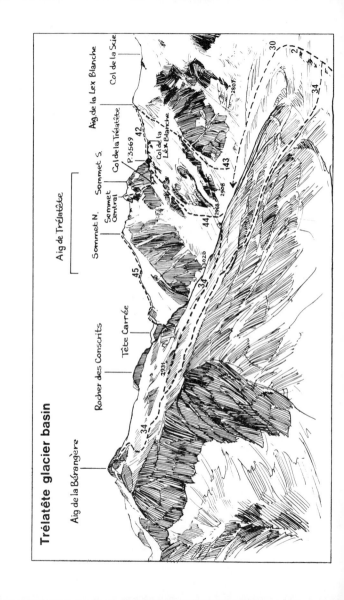

Aig de la Bérangère

Rocher des Conscrits

Tête Carrée

Aig de Trélatête

Sommet N.

Sommet Central

Sommet S.

Col de la Trélatête

Aig. de la Lex Blanche

Col de la Lex Blanche

Col de la Scie

P.3569

2807

34

2

30

143

42

441

44

45

3.4

3.4

2920

2964

2988

2931

COL DE LA LEX BLANCHE 3555m.

COL DE TRÉLATÊTE 3515m.

See Routes 42 and 44.

AIGUILLE DE TRÉLATÊTE 3930m. 3920m. IGM

"By far the most important peak as well as the highest at the
south-west end of the chain" (Whymper). This complex mtn.
has four distinct summits rising on a ridge about 900m. long
and curving from E to N. The normal routes are superior
glacier and snow climbs of their class, and while technical
problems are not great all of them must be regarded as serious
expeditions.
    The summits so formed are: E Peak (3895m., a snow cap),
S Peak or SE Centrale (3930m., the highest pt.), Central Peak
or NW Centrale (3917m., situated at a junction with the frontier
ridge), and N Peak or Tête Blanche (3892m.).
    First ascents: E and S Peaks: A. A. Reilly and Ed. Whymper
with Michel Croz, M. Payot and H. Charlet, 12 July, 1864.
Central Peak: M. Baretti with J. J. Maquignaz, A. and V.
Sibille, 8 August, 1878. N. Peak: A. W. Moore and Horace
Walker with Jakob Anderegg and J. Jaun, 23 July, 1870.
    N Peak ascended on ski by Armand Charlet and Camille
Dévouassoud, 23 May, 1926.

French Side

Central and South Peaks via Cols de la Lex Blanche and
Trélatête. The easiest route to the highest summits from the
Trélatête side.   Varied glacier and snow work, and rock
climbing. A fine expedition, PD+/AD. From the Col de Tré-
latête, first ascensionists of Central Peak.   To Col de
Trélatête, Messrs. Averton, Bullock, Hopworth and Irving,
August, 1923.

44 From the Trélatête hotel follow Routes 2, 30 to a point on
the glacier about 15 min. above the level of the Conscrits hut.
Slant across to the R side of the glacier and move up to a snow
slope in a large bay to the L of rock spur pt. 2968 (3 h.).
Cross a bergschrund which slants L up the bay, and ascend on

a diagonal line, steep snow, between the bergschrund and a rockband above. In 15 min., still close to the bergschrund, more continuous broken rocks rise towards Pt. 3569 on the main ridge. This pt. lies between the Col de la Lex Blanche (R) and Col de Trélatête (L). Climb these broken rocks, mixed with snow, to an upper section on more continuous snow. At a fairly obvious rock patch in this slant L up a snow crest to reach the main ridge L of Pt. 3569 and go along the easy rock crest to the Col de Trélatête (2½ h.).

Above the col is the SW ridge of Central Peak. A snow crest leads to a rock buttress which is climbed somewhat R of the ridge to its top, pt. 3660. In good conditions it is now best to continue up a fine corniced snow crest to a steep rock rib which leads without particular difficulty to the summit ridge just L of the Central Peak (2 h.). An alternative to the fine snow crest and rock rib consists of climbing steep snow slopes and a few rocks further R, finishing up a couloir just R of the rib to the summit. PD/PD+ to this point.

The most delicate part of the expedition is the short ridge linking the Central and S Peaks. From the former a rock spine then a very narrow snow crest, normally with awkward cornices, leads to the latter (15 min. in good conditions, 7¾ h. from Trélatête hotel, 5½ h. from Conscrits hut).

North Ridge of North Peak (Tête Blanche). A frequented route; in poor conditions the slopes are prone to avalanche. F+. Continuation from the N Peak to Central Peak is a more serious proposition. First ascent: L. Kraul, W. Martin, E. Meyer and R. Weitzenböck, 17 August, 1912.

45 From the Trélatête hotel follow Routes 2, 30 to within 600m. distance of Col Infranchissable (about 4 h.). On the R (SE) a snowy rock rib comes down from the frontier ridge about 100m. R of the Tête Carrée summit. Cross the glacier and climb this rib on moderately steep and loose rocks with snow to the main ridge ($1\frac{1}{4}$ h.). Now follow the main ridge over a slight saddle on snow and occasional rocks, avoiding cornices possibly on both sides, to finish up a steep snow slope at the N Peak (45 min., 6 h. from Trélatête hotel, $3\frac{3}{4}$ h. from Conscrits hut).

The continuation ridge (same first ascensionists) to the Central Peak is AD, involving narrow corniced crests, several gendarmes traversed or turned on good and bad rock, and steep verglassed rocks ($1\frac{3}{4}$ h.).

Italian Side

Note: Several routes joining or coming close to the two described below have been practised by parties setting out from the Elisabetta hut. These routes involve variable approaches up the lower part of the Lex Blanche glacier which is normally badly crevassed and cut by large icefalls. These approaches are not recommended except when the glacier is in exceptionally good condition.

South Ridge of East Peak - South Peak.
The normal route from the Estelette biv. Conditions on the middle part of the Lex Blanche glacier vary considerably. PD/PD+. First ascent: F. Gonella with A. Berthod and J. Petigax, 28 July, 1887.

46 From the biv. follow Route 40 to the snow saddle at the foot of the steep part of the SE ridge of the Aig. des Glaciers (1 h.). Now descend across a snow slope R to the Lex Blanche glacier and traverse crevassed slopes R (N) to the rock barrier forming the E ridge of the Aig. de la Lex Blanche. Climb this easily by broken rocks just R of pt. 3300; work R to avoid stonefall. So reach the upper branch of the glacier; descend slightly to the NE along the top of an icefall to reach the flank of the S ridge ahead (1 h.). In this flank below and just R of pt. 3459 is a couloir. L of the couloir a weakness runs up to the ridge still R of pt. 3459. From the glacier climb this weakness, a sort of gutter, first on the R, then in a narrow bed, to the crest of the S ridge (1 h.). Follow the ridge on generally easy rocks over pts. 3459 and 3537 to a shoulder, then steeper moderately difficult rocks on the upper rib to a small shoulder at the base of the summit step 60m. above. From here the original route traverses L to cross steep snow forming the top of a broad hanging glacier couloir, between the S ridges of the E and S Peaks. Slant up gradually to finish on the ridge connecting the two peaks just below the S top; there is often a large cornice here. A short snow slope leads to the summit ($1\frac{1}{2}$-2 h., $4\frac{3}{4}$-5 h. from Estelette biv.).

Finishing up the S ridge direct to the E Peak is grade III, from where the linking ridge corresponds with Route 47.

<u>South-East Side of East Peak - South Peak.</u> The easiest route of all, the one taken by Whymper's party. In the last 10 years probably more frequented than all other routes put together. Generally PD.

47 From the Petit Mt. Blanc biv. (3047m.) climb rock banks to the broad snow spur rising NW to the Petit Mt. Blanc and follow the L side of the crest line to the top (3424m.) ($1\frac{1}{2}$ h.). F. Down to the L (SW) from the summit, descend a 40m. rockband by a couloir and easy rocks to the Petit Mt. Blanc glacier. Make a rising traverse W across the glacier, under the Aig. de l'Aigle and continue NW to a bergschrund and head-slope leading to the ENE spur of the E Peak at a shoulder. In good conditions a more direct line to the L (W) can be taken to the spur, up a couloir-like slope close to pt. 3644. Climb the spur, narrowing to a fine snow ridge, to the E Peak ($2\frac{1}{2}$ h.). The ridge running to the S Peak normally has a large cornice on the L (S) side. Traverse it keeping R, cross a bergschrund and finish up a snow slope to the S Peak (45 min., $4\frac{3}{4}$ h. from Petit Mt. Blanc biv.).

PETIT MONT BLANC 3424m.

Superb regional viewpoint for those based at Courmayeur, and classic panorama of SW side of Mont Blanc. Frequently visited from its biv. hut (q. v.). See Route 47 (1½ h.). No record of parties climbing the Aig. de Trélatête actually crossing the summit before: G. Bobba with C. Thérisod and M. Bognier, 4 August, 1897.

TÊTE CARRÉE 3732m.

A good viewpoint above Col Infranchissable. On reaching the main ridge by Route 45, climb L to the top in a few min. (5½ h. from Trélatête hotel, 3 h. from Conscrits hut).

COL DE MIAGE 3342m.

Between the Dômes de Miage Pt. 3672m. and the Aig. de Bionnassay. Rarely used as a pass, but both sides climbed often enough to reach the Durier hut situated just below the saddle near its N end. Invariably associated with climbing the Aig. de Bionnassay. Both sides PD, somewhat long and tedious. See Routes 3 and 4. First recorded tourist traverse: E. T. Coleman with F. Mollard and two others, 11 September, 1858.

AIGUILLE DE BIONNASSAY 4052m.

At Chamonix in 1865, "the only peak passing 13,000 ft. which had escaped the devastations of the Alpine Club" (Grove). A beautiful and picturesque satellite of Mt. Blanc, situated to the W of the parent mtn. All the routes are splendid snow/ice climbs, serious in nature, and demanding a degree of experience. Traversed fairly often to Mt. Blanc. The summit is a knife blade of snow.

First ascent: E. N. Buxton, F. C. Grove and R. J. S. Macdonald with J.-P. Cachet and M. Payot, 28 July, 1865. First winter ascent: Armand Charlet and R. Frison-Roche; H. Hoerlin, E. Schneider and H. Schroder, 20 March, 1929.

<u>South Ridge.</u> The normal route, a splendid ridge, PD+ on the rock step in average conditions. First ascent: G. Gruber

with K. Maurer and A. Jaun, 13 July, 1888. This party avoided the rock step by a traverse on the SE side. Climbed directly by Miss K. Richardson with Emile Rey and J.-B. Bich, 13 August, 1888.

48 From the Durier hut (3349m.) on the Col de Miage ascend the broad snow ridge to the N. Cross a shoulder (3619m.) where the ridge narrows, then go up rocks over another narrow snow shoulder (3810m.) with small cornices to a delicate horizontal section leading to the rock step. A zone of smooth slabs runs R-wards along the base of the step. Climb these R of the crest and continue about 15m. below the crest up short icy chimneys connected by small ledges to rejoin the crest at the top of the step. Alternatively, in conditions of bad verglas, it can be easier to traverse L and upwards into a steep, narrow snow couloir and follow this to the top. Also, the R side of the step has been frequently taken. Traverse snow horizontally, keeping low, and cross the ends of slabby ribs divided by shallow couloirs, till a steep plain snowband (50°) can be climbed trending R. Continue R-wards up rocks through a funnel in a rockband and up more snow to rejoin the crest above the top of the step (AD). Above the step a fine snow crest runs up to the final snow slope which leads steeply to a thin snow/ice ridge forming the summit (4 h. on average).

East Ridge. The easiest route from the Gonella (Dôme) hut. A fine ridge, normally very delicate due to large cornices. AD. The approach is also the normal route to Mt. Blanc from this hut. The ridge was first done by the Richardson party in 1888 (See Route 48).

49 From the Gonella hut (3071m.) follow a track to the Dôme glacier and work up the séracs near the L side. Then go up the centre of the glacier, turning numerous crevasses, to below a division at c. 3400m. Ascend the L-hand (W) branch, flowing between the Aigs. Grises and a rock spur marked pt. 4051. It is usually best to slant L (W) to reach the Col des Aig. Grises (3810m.) by a steep snow slope. From here turn a rock outcrop on the L and follow the snow crest to a shoulder (4002m.) on the main frontier ridge above the Col de Bionnassay (3888m.) ($3\frac{1}{2}$ h.).

Now descend the steep and narrow main ridge across the Col de Bionnassay and go up the very thin E ridge of the mtn., steepening towards the top with continuous overhanging cornices. Little ice pitches and rock outcrops are turned on one flank or the other, always delicately and in an exposed position (2 h., $5\frac{1}{2}$ h. from Gonella hut).

North-West Face. A classic route and one of the finest snow/ ice climbs of its class in the Alps. 1050m., average angle 40-45°, AD/AD+. Rarely climbed before 1930, now virtually used as a normal route by Chamonix-based parties. Conditions and glacier problems vary from year to year. Study the face well the day before climbing it.

Contrary to previous reports the Grove-Buxton party (first ascensionists) did not climb the NW face. They ascended some distance R of the NW face "ribbon" and joined the Tricot (W) ridge at a small saddle just behind the Aig. de Tricot (3665m.). The party crossed an initial rockband R of pt. 3181, and their line above that corresponds with the N flank of the Aig. de Tricot. The "second ascensionists" therefore made the first direct route up the NW face ribbon: R. W. Lloyd with A. and J. Pollinger, 18 July, 1926. Subsequent parties avoided the direct finish by moving R on to the Tricot ridge, though well above the saddle behind the Aig. de Tricot.

First winter ascent: R. Simond (solo), 29 January, 1964. Descended on ski by Sylvain Saudan, 6 October, 1969 in $2\frac{1}{4}$ h. (repeated several times since, best time 55 min.).

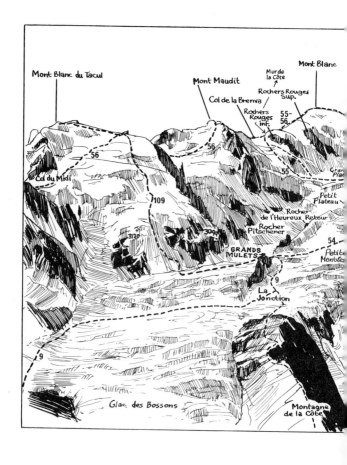

Mont Blanc du Tacul

Mont Maudit

Col de la Brenva

Mur de la Côte

Mont Blanc

Rochers Rouges Sup.

Rochers Rouges inf.

55-56

56

55

Gran Plat

Col du Midi

56

109

Petit Plateau

3730

30

Rocher de l'Heureux Retour

Rocher Pitschner

GRANDS MULETS

54

Petite Montée

9

La Jonction

Glac. des Bossons

Montagne de la Côte

9

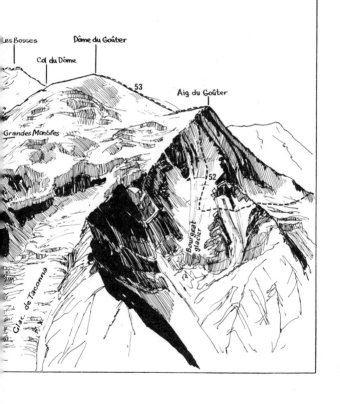

MONT BLANC N side

Les Bosses

Dôme du Goûter

Col du Dôme

53

Aig. du Goûter

Grandes Montées

52

Bourgeat glacier

Glac. de Taconna

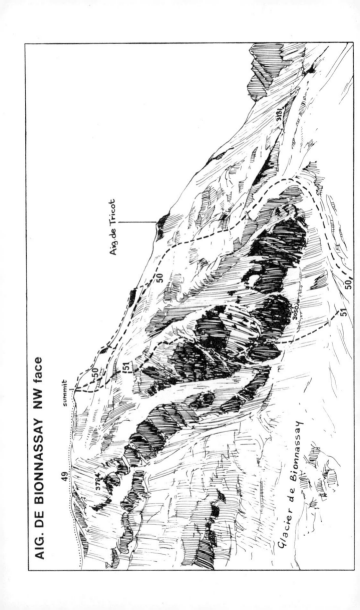

AIG. DE BIONNASSAY NW face

Aig. de Tricot

Glacier de Bionnassay

summit

49

50

50

50,

51

51

3784

3050

3181

50 From the Tête Rousse hut (3167m.) descend the steep and narrow snow slope situated below the hut to the SW (crevasses possible), and cross the scree that runs out on to the Bionnassay glacier beside pt. 2959. Climb for a few min. along the L side of the glacier, then traverse (crevasses in same direction) to the base of a huge glacier ribbon, supported by ice cliffs and a rock barrier, which descends from the neighbourhood of the summit below the Tricot ridge. Traverse R on to the ribbon and climb it as directly as possible (45°). There are ice bosses, walls and crevasses to overcome or circumvent, with short pitches at 50-55° possible. Normally the upper section is taken by a movement to the R. Aim for the Tricot ridge up on the R at c. 3750m., about level with the first of two rock spines on this ridge above the Aig. de Tricot. The ridge can be joined here (easiest way) and followed over a second rock spine to the steep terminal ridge and the summit. Alternatively, continue on the face below the ridge and join the latter by a traverse R to the base of the second rock spine. The proper way is a direct ascent on the upper part of the face; move L away from the ridge, cross a bergschrund and climb trending L then R at 45° to the summit - steeper and harder than the ridge (4-8 h. from Tête Rousse hut).

51 <u>North-West Face, Central Route.</u> This route was described with reasonable accuracy in the previous guide. However the difficulty was overrated and is probably about D. It appears to be an unattractive route on poor rock with little character and no protection, while the upper ice pitches might need a lot of pegging or become impossible. Repeated once and not recommended. First ascent: B. Kempf and C. Laurendeau, 30-31 August, 1953. Another route was put up further L in July, 1975.

<u>Traverse of Frontier Ridge to Mont Blanc.</u> Starting from the Durier hut (Col de Miage), a traverse of the Aig. de Bionnassay

by the S and E ridges (Routes 48, 49) can be continued across the Col de Bionnassay by the SW ridge of the Dôme du Goûter to Mont Blanc (Route 58). This makes a magnificent expedition, one of the finest ridge traverses in the Alps. It can be made more interesting and longer by starting from the Trélatête hotel and traversing the Dômes de Miage to the Durier hut. In good conditions, AD. The time from the Durier hut to the summit of Mt. Blanc could vary from 8 to 13 h. First traverse: Capt. J. P. Farrar with D. Maquignaz and J. Kederbacher, 16 August, 1898.

COL DE BIONNASSAY   3888m.

Between the Aig. de Bionnassay and Dôme du Goûter. Not of any value as a pass. French side, very dangerous, D. Italian side, PD/PD+. Traversed only once: R. W. Lloyd with J. and A. Pollinger, 14 August, 1919.

AIGUILLES GRISES

Numerous rock summits forming the ridge coming down from the frontier at pt. 4002 near the Col de Bionnassay, and dividing the It. Bionnassay glacier (W) and Dôme glacier (E). The Gonella hut is situated below them on the Dôme glacier side. Parties staying at this hut have made several good training climbs on these summits; the rock is generally good. See Route 59.

DÔME DU GOÛTER   4304m.

The large snow hump traversed or contoured by the normal route up Mt. Blanc.

AIGUILLE DU GOÛTER   3863m.

The prominent snow crest running along the top of an escarpment of numerous and regular looking rock ribs and couloirs which prefaces many views of Mt. Blanc from the valley. The proximity of the Goûter hut (3817m.) at the top of the escarpment ensures that the summit is crossed frequently by parties going up Mt. Blanc. The ordinary route corresponds with the hut approach from the Tête Rousse (Route 8). The escarpment and its features are associated with poor rock and bad stonefall. Ascended before 1784 by two Chamoniards. Couloirs on the NW side have been skied down at least three times since 1970.

North Face. This triangular face rises out of the much reduced Bourgeat glacier. By traversing on to the glacier face from the W, a practical and interesting snow/ice climb can be made. 800m., AD, some stonefall possible. Compared by André Contamine for quality with the N face of the Aig. d'Argentière. First ascent: P. Labrunie, M. Vaucher, A. Contamine, P. Julien and Y. Pollet-Villard, 7 July, 1957.

52 From the Tête Rousse hut (3167m.) descend the hut approach path (Route 6) till a convenient short descent can be made to the Griaz glacier. Cross the rubble, snow and ice on this easy glacier horizontally ENE, then cross the NW ridge of the mtn. just above pt. 2912. Continue traversing generally snowy rock ribs and reach the glacier face by a steep traverse (1 h.). Start up the centre, crossing two bergschrunds, and higher up trend slightly L into a couloir. Climb this for a short way then exit R up a series of short loose rock steps (delicate) to finish on snow and the crest running towards the Goûter hut (2¼ h., 3¼ h. from hut on first ascent).

Mont Blanc

MONT BLANC   4807m.

The highest summit in the Alps. A complex and beautiful
mountain with six major ridges - the Bosses, Mt. Maudit,
Peuterey, Innominata, Brouillard and Bionnassay. These
ridges and especially the faces between them provide the most
interesting and varied collection of routes to any summit in
the Alps. Important secondary peaks crossed by routes which
lead to the summit of Mont Blanc are Mont Blanc de Courmayeur (4748m.), Picco Luigi Amedeo (4460m.), Dôme du
Goûter (4304m.), and the Aig. du Goûter (3863m.). For the
purpose of this guide, the limits of the mountain are defined
as the cols of Bionnassay (3888m.), Brenva (4303m.), Peuterey
(3934m.), Eccles (4041m.), and Emile Rey (4030m.). The
satellite peaks of Mont Blanc, beyond these cols, are described in other sections of the guide.

Apart from the intrinsic difficulties of any of the routes,
there are all the dangers inherent in any long expedition at
high altitude. Great care and judgement must be exercised at
all times. In bad weather, climbing on Mont Blanc is particularly dangerous, especially on ridges exposed to wind.
Route finding in poor visibility is made unusually difficult by
the complex structure of the mtn. and its glacier systems.
Compass bearings are unreliable as the needle is often affected
by magnetic rock. In event of bad weather, the only recommended route for descent is the Bosses ridge and the Grand
Plateau, or possibly over the Aig. du Goûter.

First ascent: Dr. M. G. Paccard and Jacques Balmat, 8
August, 1786. In winter: Miss I. Straton with J. Charlet and
S. Couttet, 31 January, 1876. On ski: H. Mylius with
A. Tännler, K. Maurer and H. Zurflüh, 25 February, 1904.
Traversed on ski: R. von Tscharner and M. Wieland, 20
April, 1924.

Normal routes from Chamonix

<u>Goûter (Bosses) Ridge</u>. The best route of ascent, offering
little in the way of technical difficulty in good weather and
conditions. A classic expedition with magnificent views. F+
in normal conditions, but in bad snow conditions dangerous and
tiring.

Above the Goûter hut, the route is exposed to wind. Route finding on the broad slopes between the Dôme and the Bosses ridge can be very tricky in cloud. Note the position of the Vallot hut, as one approaches the Bosses ridge, in case of emergency during descent. First complete ascent: Leslie Stephen and F. F. Tuckett with Melchior Anderegg, J. J. Bennen and Peter Perren, 18 July 1861.

53 From the Goûter hut (3817m.) climb a short steep snow slope to the crest of the Aig. du Goûter. Traverse the broad snow ridge to the SE towards the Dôme du Goûter (4304m.), which is flat and indistinct. Avoid the Dôme on the R (S) side, about 200m. from the apparent summit. Continue descending slightly to the broad saddle of the Col du Dôme. Keep going more or less in the same direction towards the Bosses ridge. The Vallot hut (4362m.) is on a small prominent rock about 150m. to the L (3 h.). The slope narrows, steepens and merges into the Bosses ridge. Continue up the broad ridge over two prominent snow humps, the Grande Bosse (4513m.) and the Petite Bosse (4547m.). Descend into a slight dip, then continue keeping to the L of the Rochers de la Tournette (4677m.) and finally go up a well defined snow ridge to the summit (2 h., 5 h. from the Goûter hut).

The summit is formed by a broad snow ridge, nearly horizontal for about 50m. and orientated E–W. If time and weather allow, it is worth following the narrow ridge to the S to Mt. Blanc de Courmayeur (4748m.), for a view over the Italian precipices ($\frac{1}{2}$-1 h.).

<u>Grands Mulets Route (by the Grand Plateau and Bosses Ridge)</u>.
Traditionally the most reliable route to the summit; more sheltered than the Goûter route, but only in the lower section. The ascent to the Col du Dôme is rather tedious, with long slopes broken by many crevasses and exposed to falling séracs. The guides sometimes place ladders across large crevasses.

In fine weather a broad trail will be found in the snow. F+ in normal conditions. First complete ascent: E. Headland, G. C. Hodgkinson, C. Hudson and G. C. Joad with F. Couttet and two other guides, 29 July, 1859.

54 From the Grands Mulets hut (3051m.) climb the glacier in a SW direction towards some rocks jutting out from the N ridge of the Dôme, keeping to a diagonal line to avoid the worst crevasses. Near the ice cliffs of the Dôme, climb a steep snow slope on the L (the Petites Montées) to a small shelf, the Petit Plateau, c. 3650m. (2 h.). Cross the shelf, keeping as far away as possible from the ice cliffs of the Dôme on the R. Climb another steep snow slope, the Grandes Montées, and at the top of this cross the large crevasse on the R to reach a large snowfield, the Grand Plateau, c. 3950m. Traverse this towards the SW then go up a long slope to the W to reach the Col du Dôme ($2\frac{1}{4}$ h.). Now join Route 53 to the summit ($2\frac{1}{4}$ h., $6\frac{1}{2}$ h. from Grands Mulets hut).

When the Petites Montées slope is badly crevassed, it can be avoided by keeping close to the snow/rock crest of the Rocher Pitschner and the Rocher de l'Heureux Retour, to the L of the normal route, until the Petit Plateau can be reached by a traverse to the R.

Corridor Route. One of the classic routes of Mt. Blanc and as easy as any, F+. It is ascended much less frequently than the other routes. In bad weather it should be avoided, above all for descent. The correct and best line is precise and landmarks are absent. First ascent: C. Fellows and W. Hawes with Mathieu and Michel Balmat, J. M. and P. M. Couttet, S. Dévouassoud, M. Favret, D. Folliguet, J. Payot and P. J. Simond, 25 July, 1827.

55 From the Grands Mulets hut follow Route 54 as far as the lower end of the Grand Plateau ($3\frac{1}{4}$ h.). Cross the snowfield in an ESE direction, to a rocky rognon (3928m.) encircled by séracs, at the foot of the Corridor, which is a snowy valley, sandwiched between the Rochers Rouges (R) and the NW ridge of Mt. Maudit (L). There are two ways of climbing the Corridor:

(i) Between the lower Rochers Rouges (4290) and the Rognon: this way is slightly exposed to falling séracs and possibly snow avalanches on the lower part of the Corridor slopes. The route finding is easy because the wall of the Rochers Rouges on the R makes an excellent boundary. Normally this route is quicker than the L-hand alternative.

(ii) Between the rognon and Mt. Maudit: less exposed to avalanches, but more complex route finding in crevasses between two sérac barriers.

Having climbed the Corridor slopes, there is no point going up to the Col de la Brenva (4303m., huge cornices on the Brenva side). Instead, trend R (S) and go straight to the foot of the Mur de la Côte, a steep narrow snow slope, about 90m. high, between the upper Brenva séracs and the lower Rochers Rouges ($1\frac{1}{2}$ h.).

Climb the Mur de la Côte, till above the lower Rochers Rouges and continue up the slopes forming the NNE ridge of Mt. Blanc. Pass the Petits Rochers Rouges (4577m.) and the Petits Mulets (4690m.) on the L (SE) side and thence to the summit ($2\frac{1}{4}$ h., 7 h. from the Grands Mulets hut).

Descent via Mont Maudit to the Col du Midi. A fine traverse, though long and tiring and thus better taken in descent. PD. Two wooden stakes should be carried for abseiling over bergschrunds. In normal conditions, this route is neither difficult nor dangerous, but in certain conditions Mt. Maudit and Mt. Blanc du Tacul can have slopes in serious danger of avalanching. The route is often combined with the Bosses ridge, giving a classic traverse of Mt. Blanc. It can also be combined with

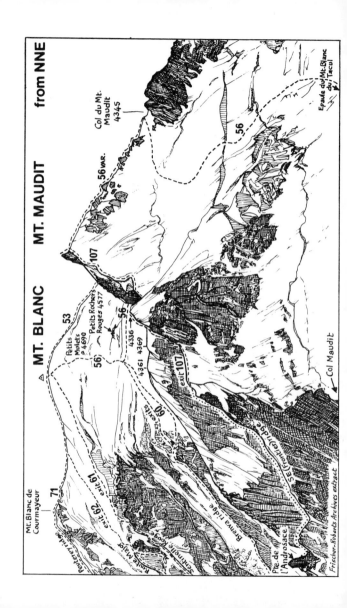

△ **MT. BLANC** **MT. MAUDIT** from NNE

Mt. Blanc de Courmayeur

71

Peuterey ridge

exit 62 exit 61

60 exit

Route Major

Sentinelle route

Brenva ridge

Pte. de l'Androsace

SE (frontier ridge)

Col Maudit

Petits Mulets 4690

53

Petits Rochers Rouges 4577

56

4336

4369

4361

exit 107

56

56 var.

107

Col du Mt. Maudit 4345

56

Epaule du Mt. Blanc du Tacul

Frischer-Roberts Archives extract

the traverse of the Aig. de Bionnassay or even the Dômes de Miage. See note at end of entry on Aig. de Bionnassay. First complete ascent of this route: R. W. Head with J. Grange, A. Orset and J.-M. Perrod, 13 August, 1863.

56 From the summit of Mt. Blanc descend the NNE ridge, passing to the R (SE) of the rock outcrops of the Petits Mulets and the Petits Rochers Rouges. Continue down the 90m. slope of the Mur de la Côte to just N of the Col de la Brenva (4303m.). Traverse the W slopes of Mt. Maudit, keeping below the summit, to reach the Col du Mt. Maudit (4345m.) in the NW ridge of that mtn. Or, from the Col de la Brenva, one can climb the easy S ridge of Mt. Maudit (4465m.) to the summit and descend the rocky NW ridge to the Col du Mt. Maudit. This detour adds 1 h.

From the col descend steeply to the N. There is normally a wide bergschrund, crossed on the extreme L or R. Wooden stake for abseiling useful. Reach the broad snowy cwm between Mt. Maudit and Mt. Blanc du Tacul. Contour across this, then go up slightly to reach the broad W ridge of Mt. Blanc du Tacul, some distance W of its summit. From here one can easily climb to the summit of Mt. Blanc du Tacul (4248m.) in about 30 min. From here descend the steep broken snow slopes cut by crevasses and small sérac barriers (zigzag) with a final large bergschrund at the bottom (fixed ladders often in place) to the Col du Midi (3532m.) (5-7 h. from the summit, excluding diversions).

From the Col du Midi, one can either traverse under the SE face of the Aig. du Midi and go up to the cableway station, or descend to the Requin hut via the Vallée Blanche or the Géant glacier.

Normal routes from Courmayeur

Rocher du Mont Blanc Route. A direct and elegant route,

recommended for its pleasant climbing and good views, PD. Somewhat exposed to stonefall. It is advisable to descend as early as possible in the day. First ascent: T. S. Kennedy with J.-A. Carrel and J. Fischer, 2 July, 1872. The first winter traverse of Mt. Blanc was made by this route (descending by Route 54) by the three Sella bros. and 6 guides and porters, 5 January, 1888.

57 From the Quintino Sella hut (3371m.) there are two ways of starting:

(i) Climb a little glacier to the NE, on steep slopes at first and with numerous crevasses, to reach a snowy saddle at the SE foot of the Rocher du Mont Blanc ($1\frac{1}{2}$ h.).

(ii) Alternatively, to avoid the crevasses, a longer route consists of traversing the glacier just above the level of the hut, then scrambling up a prominent rocky crest on the R (S) side of the glacier, until it gives on to snow below the saddle ($1\frac{3}{4}$ h.).

From the saddle, descend to the upper plateau of the Mt. Blanc glacier. Cross the glacier to the N to reach the lower S extremity of the rocks that rise above the glacier, towards the Rochers de la Tournette on the Bosses ridge (4677m.). The lower part of these rocks form a large wall, whose base slopes sharply up to the L. Higher up the wall merges into a snowy shoulder, which merges with the Bosses ridge.

Cross the bergschrund, sometimes difficult, and climb to the R in a little snowy couloir, or by the rocks bordering it, to reach a ridge that marks the SE side of the wall. Climb the ridge easily, on steep shattered rocks, turning obstacles on the R side. Higher up, continue by the snow ridge, crossing several rock outcrops. Turn the last outcrop (c. 4500m.) on the R and then make a diagonal ascent to reach the Bosses ridge, just above the Rochers de la Tournette. Follow the ridge to the summit (5 h., $6\frac{1}{2}$-8 h. from the Quintino Sella hut, 5 h. in descent).

<u>Grises Route by the Dôme Glacier</u>. The easiest and shortest route from Courmayeur, PD. Fairly complicated route finding, and the glacier is normally badly crevassed. It is the only completely comfortable route of descent on this side of Mt. Blanc, but in bad weather is not as safe as the Chamonix routes. First descent: L. and J. Bonin and A. Ratti (Pope Pious XI) with J. Gadin and A. Proment, 1 August, 1890.

58 From the Gonella hut (3071m.) follow Route 49 to pt. 4002 on the SW ridge of the Dôme du Goûter ($3\frac{1}{2}$ h.).

Continue up the narrow, probably corniced ridge towards the Dôme, crossing another shoulder (4153m.). At the top traverse R below the Dôme summit, then trend L (E) and cross the Col du Dôme to join Route 53 to the Bosses ridge and the summit ($3\frac{1}{2}$ h., 7 h. from the Gonella hut, 4 h. in descent).

When descending the hut is invisible. Stay on the glacier down to a small glacier plateau, opposite the foot of a narrow couloir on the L (E) coming from the gap in which the Quintino Sella hut is situated. From the plateau traverse off R to broken rocks which lead to the Gonella hut.

<u>Aiguilles Grises Ridge</u>. A variation on Route 58, which avoids the crevassed section of the Dôme glacier. Useful at the end of the season and probably shorter then than the glacier route. Interesting scrambling. PD. First ascent: R. L. G. Irving, solo, 7 August, 1919, as far as the Dôme du Goûter.

59 From the Gonella hut climb to the NW across easy snow and rock slopes, to reach the ridge of the Aigs. Grises. Follow the ridge easily over minor pts. 3367, 3409 and 3591 to a double gendarme (3606 VT) which is traversed to a third (3671); avoid this by descending for a short way in a couloir on the L side. Return to the ridge, now snow, and reach the Calotte des Aigs. Grises (3817m.). Descend a broad snow crest to the Col des Aigs. Grises (4 h.). From the col follow Route 58 to the summit (8 h. from the Gonella hut, $4\frac{1}{2}$ h. in descent).

MONT BLANC
Brenva face

Mont Blanc
de Courmayeur

Mont Blanc

71

63

62

61

60

4349
The Peak 63

62

Twisting Rib

61

Great Couloir

BRENVA RIDGE

The
Sentinelle
Rouge

63

61

60

Upper Plateau
of the Brenva Glacier

Col Moore

60

Brenva Face routes

The Brenva face is one of the largest and most beautiful in the Alps. It extends for 1.5 km. from the Brenva Ridge to the Peuterey Ridge, consisting of a complex system of couloirs, ice arêtes and rock buttresses, which become steeper and more difficult as one progresses towards the Grand Pilier d'Angle. Access to all the routes is via Col Moore (3479m. VT), at the foot of the Brenva Ridge, which is easily reached from either the Col de la Fourche or Trident huts or the Brenva bivouac. The vertical interval from Col Moore to the summit of Mont Blanc is c. 1300m. Since the climbs face directly into the morning sun, it is essential to start several hours before dawn, so as to be established on the face before sunrise.

Brenva Ridge. Distinguished by T. Graham Brown during exploration of the face as the "Old Brenva Route". This is the easiest route on the face, taking the well defined ridge which rises from Col Moore to the NNE ridge of Mt. Blanc. The difficulties are mainly those of a great snow and ice climb and can vary a lot. AD+/D. The wall of séracs at the top usually forms the crux, though in some conditions it can be quite easy. Being on a ridge, the route is easy to follow and there is little objective danger. First ascent: G. S. Mathews, A. W. Moore, F. and H. Walker, with J. and M. Anderegg, 15 July, 1865. The first route to be made on the Italian side of Mt. Blanc. First winter ascent: J. Couzy and A. Vialatte, 26 February, 1956. First solo: L. Gasparotto, 6 August, 1933. Descended on ski by Heini Holzer, 30 June, 1973.

60 To reach the upper plateau of the Brenva glacier, from the Fourche hut reverse the last part of Route 24, from the Trident hut - the last part of Route 26. From the Brenva biv. as for Route 24. On the glacier contour round towards Col Moore, at the foot of the prominent spur that sweeps down on the W of the glacier. A short steep snow slope leads to the col (1 h. from Fourche, 45 min. from Trident, $1\frac{3}{4}$ h. from Brenva biv.).

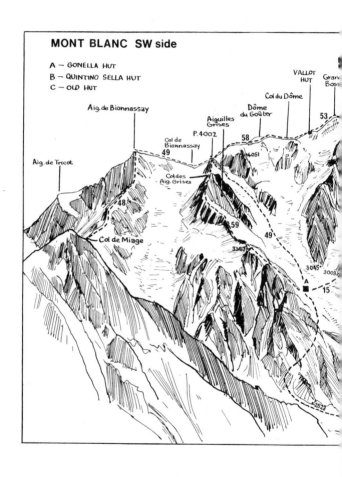

MONT BLANC SW side

A — GONELLA HUT
B — QUINTINO SELLA HUT
C — OLD HUT

VALLOT HUT

Gran Boss

Col du Dôme

Aig. de Bionnassay

Dôme du Goûter

Aiguilles Grises

Col de Bionnassay
49

P. 4002

53

58

4051

Col des Aig. Grises

Aig. de Tricot

48

59

Col de Miage

3367

49

3045

3003

A

15

2525

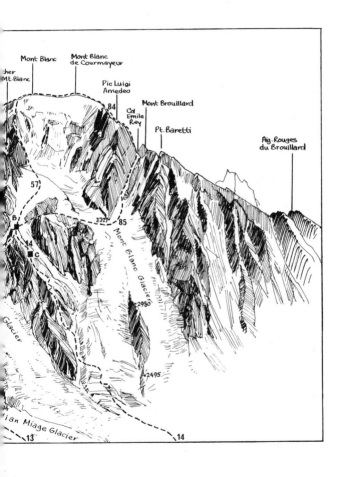

Mont Blanc

cier
Mt. Blanc

Mont Blanc
de Courmayeur

Pic Luigi
Amedeo

84

Col
Emile
Rey

Mont Brouillard

Pt. Baretti

Aig. Rouges
du Brouillard

57

B

85

3327

14
C

Mont Blanc Glacier

2930

2495

Glacier

ian Miage Glacier

13

14

From Col Moore follow the snowy ridge to a little step, which is avoided on the L. Continue up the ridge to a large rock buttress, with a 45° rake slanting up to the L. Follow this rake and then easy rocks lead back to the main ridge, above the buttress. Follow the crest of the rocky ridge until it narrows to the famous ice ridge which is usually snow (2 h.). Follow the ice ridge, cornices possible, and continue up the long snow or ice slopes above, possibly crevassed, keeping roughly in line with the rocks defining the ridge on the R. This leads to the foot of the highest rocks on the ridge. Turn these on the L, usually by an ice pitch and reach two small rock fingers. The terminal sérac band runs some distance above.

Moore exit. Only used when the other two look very difficult or impossible. Descend or rope down the steep snow/ice/ rock flank of the ridge to jumbled ice ledges running N below the cliffs. At the end go up short ice steps into a hollow and climb diagonally R out of this to finish above the Mur de la Côte.

Coolidge exit. Climb steep ice above, trending R with variable features into an ice gully which normally leads out somewhat R through a breach in the cliffs.

Direct exit. In favourable conditions traverse delicately L and climb a steep snow/ice slope between the séracs to the top.

$4\frac{1}{2}$ h. from ice ridge, $6\frac{1}{2}$ h. from Col Moore. Join Route 55 and reach the summit of Mt. Blanc in another $1\frac{1}{4}$ h.

Sentinelle Rouge. A splendid route, leading directly to the summit of Mt. Blanc. Slightly steeper and harder than the Brenva Ridge, but again the difficulties are variable; D/D+. The traverse of the Great Couloir is exposed to avalanches and must be crossed before dawn. It is possible to bivouac at the Sentinelle Rouge, but it is usually better to start from the Fourche/Trident huts. First ascent: T. Graham Brown and

F. S. Smythe, 1-2 September, 1927. First winter ascent: Walter Bonatti and G. Panei, 9 March, 1961. First solo: J. Afanassief, 3 September, 1971.

61 Approach as for Route 60 to Col Moore ($\frac{3}{4}$-$1\frac{3}{4}$ h.). Follow the snow ridge above and leave it either below or just above the first little step. Traverse rising L on snow and rock, crossing four couloirs (danger of stone and ice falls from the wall of séracs above), then go up an ice slope and some rocks to a high red tower, the Sentinelle Rouge ($1\frac{1}{2}$ h., good bivouac site).

Pass the Sentinelle on the L and climb to the foot of a characteristic step, on the long rocky rib which forms the R side of the Great Couloir. Enter the couloir and climb it, first keeping close to the R side then by a long ascending traverse, to reach the foot of a buttress which splits the couloir at its widest part. This is the Twisting Rib. Climb the rib, keeping to the R at first then up the crest. Avoid a high steep step on the R and rejoin the upper part of the rib, which is usually an ice crest. Above this climb a rock wall by a diagonal chimney, leading on to the upper slopes. Climb these over snow and rock, going R at first then more or less straight up. Avoid the barrier of séracs, usually by an ice shoulder on the R side of the upper part of the Great Couloir, and reach the summit ridge (7-8 h., $8\frac{1}{2}$-$9\frac{1}{2}$ h. from Col Moore). Easy snow slopes lead to the summit in 1 h.

Route Major. Col Major is a name derived as a corruption of Courmayeur. It appears on old maps showing a pass hereabouts, long since shown to be an error for the Col de la Seigne or some neighbouring pass. Col Major, where the climb finishes, corresponds with the lowest pt. in the summit ridge between Mt. Blanc and Mt. Blanc de Courmayeur (approx. the position of la Tourette, 4741m. on map).

A route of great character; one of the finest and most important in the Alps. It is slightly less direct to the summit of Mt. Blanc than the Sentinelle Rouge, but even finer and more sustained, D/D+. Variations, which a party may be forced to use, are harder. The climb takes the long rock/ice buttress which defines the L side of the Great Couloir. It is essential to leave the Fourche/Trident huts $3\frac{1}{2}$-4 h. before dawn, so as to be across the couloir before sunrise. First ascent: T. Graham Brown and F. S. Smythe, 6-7 August, 1928. First winter ascent: Toni Gobbi and A. Ottoz, 23 March, 1953. First solo: Walter Bonatti, 10 September, 1959.

62 Follow Route 61 to beneath the Sentinelle Rouge ($1\frac{1}{2}$ h.). Slant up L to the edge of the Great Couloir, which is about 45m. wide at this point and not very steep. Cross the couloir to reach the foot of the big buttress which contains the L side. Climb the buttress to the foot of a step, near which is a thin gendarme (bivouac place). Turn this step by descending into the Great Couloir and climbing its L side, until it is possible to regain the buttress above the step. Alternatively, the top of the step can be reached by traversing the couloir at a higher level.

Continue straight up by the first short ice crest. Climb the slabs on the R, traverse L and climb some chimneys which lead to the second ice crest. This is quite long and is followed almost immediately by the third, very sharp, ice crest. Above this some rocks lead to the foot of the last and longest of the ice crests. Either climb straight up it, or traverse along its R flank to the foot of the large final buttress and go up under the rocks to reach the top of the ice crest. Climb the short first wall of the buttress by a 5m. chimney, usually choked with ice, to reach a snow covered shelf. From here there are three alternative routes up the final buttress. The first seems to be the quickest and most satisfactory, but the last is the easiest in good conditions.

(i) Continue straight up the snow/ice band above into a large corner. At the back of this is a steep chimney/couloir. Enter the chimney from the R along a big flake (III) and climb to a recess (IV) below an icy overhang. Go over this (V, pegs) and continue up the couloir bed, trending L to exit at the top of the buttress.

(ii) Ascend the ice slope diagonally L to three chimney/break lines on a frontage of c. 12m. in the rock wall. The middle one has a slab at its base. Climb this and the icy chimney above (V, pegs); or the chimney on the L and return R to the middle line (V, pegs). Continue above in cracks and a smooth groove (15m., V) to slabs, broken rocks and snow/ice leading to the top of the buttress. The R-hand chimney can also be climbed at a similar standard but is more strenuous.

(iii) Traverse R on the snow/ice slope under the buttress to a short overhanging corner, whose R wall is a rib projecting finger-like into the slope. Climb the corner by a short strenuous crack to the rib crest on the R above (III+). This corner can be very difficult when the level of ice rising into it is low. In this event it is possible to make a delicate circular movement down and round the toe of the rib to reascend on the far side.

From the rib traverse R into a snowy couloir and climb this to the foot of a long chimney/gutter. Climb the chimney keeping L for 15m. (III+), then return to the bed and follow it with a move L halfway up to reach the top of the buttress. Alternatively, start up the long chimney by stepping R and climbing another chimney of 5m., from which a traverse L is taken into the main one.

The top of the buttress lies directly below the final sérac barrier. This often constitutes the most difficult section of the climb and can take a long time. Climb the barrier, usually towards the L-hand side through the easiest break line that can be found, then go up to the summit ridge about 20 min.

from the top of Mt. Blanc (9-12 h. from Col Moore).

<u>Pear Route.</u> A magnificent climb. The hardest of the Brenva routes and one of the most exposed to objective dangers. D+. In good conditions and if the correct route is taken, it is not much harder than Route Major, but it can be much more difficult. The sections most exposed to avalanche and stonefall seem to be the slopes between the Great Couloir and the Pear; the last 30m. of the Pear; the 60m. between the last rock rognon and the final séracs. It is essential to reach the foot of the Pear before dawn. Climbed about 50 times and still infrequently compared with the other Brenva face routes. First ascent: T. Graham Brown with A. Graven and A. Aufdenblatten, 5 August, 1933. First winter ascent: A. and A. Ollier and F. Salluard, 8-9 February, 1965. First solo: C. Mauri, 13 September, 1959.

63 From Col Moore (Route 60) climb the Brenva snow ridge above and leave it either below or just above the first little step. Traverse horizontally across a couloir and several rocky ribs with intervening icy grooves to reach the large ice slope below the Great Couloir, just above the second bergschrund. Cross this ice slope (30°), rising slightly, to reach the lower rocks of the ridge line rising towards the Pear buttress (2 h.).

Climb the ridge on snow to the R then slabby rock. Continue by a snow crest then more rock. Turn a gendarme on the L, rejoin the ridge and go up to the steep lower slabs of the Pear. The buttress above is c. 275m. high. Ascend slabs trending slightly L by good ledges, a vague gully and a short chimney leading to broken rock with two short slab moves. Reach after 3-4 rope lengths a ledge at L side of face. From here climb trending R across a shallow snow couloir, then go fairly directly up the centre of the buttress by cracked rocks (III) to a pt. about 10m. below the largest (but quite small) snow patch on the face. Traverse R to a narrow couloir and climb cracks (IV) to a small notch in the vertical edge to your R, at a pt. about 40m. below the apparent top of the buttress.

Two possibilities to reach the top of the buttress:

(i) Much the shortest but very exposed on occasions to falling ice from séracs to the L. Move several m. L, climb a short wall (IV), then trend L up steep ledged rocks and cracks, working back R to the top (III and IV).

(ii) Much longer, harder but safe. From the notch follow a rising icy ledge line R, interrupted by short slabs, for 40m. (III). Now climb slabs direct for 20m. (IV), then traverse on a rising ledge line L (exposed) for 20m. From the end of this section climb another slabby wall for 8-10m. (III+) to a ledge/stance. A short exposed wall on the R (V-) leads to a third traverse line running R. Follow this for 45m. with short upward pitches, to its upper end. Climb a 8m. rib above then step R into an icy chimney and follow this with stances to the top of the buttress (IV/IV+).

From the top of the Pear take a snow crest and cross the head of an ice gully falling to the R. Beyond, a rocky rib leads up to the little Aig. de la Belle Étoile (4349m.). Turn the base of this on the L and reach the gap behind. Continue on rocks over a hump (Pointe Ultime), followed by another traverse R across a steep snow/ice couloir. Above, mixed broken ground leads to the highest rock outcrops in ice below the terminal sérac barriers.

The conventional exit is to climb a ramp formation slanting R, and by a long rising traverse on ice turn the barrier. According to conditions, considerable danger from falling ice in the first part of the movement. The ramp is sometimes ill-formed or impossible. Beyond this easy snow slopes lead to the summit ridge a short distance R of Mt. Blanc de Courmayeur.

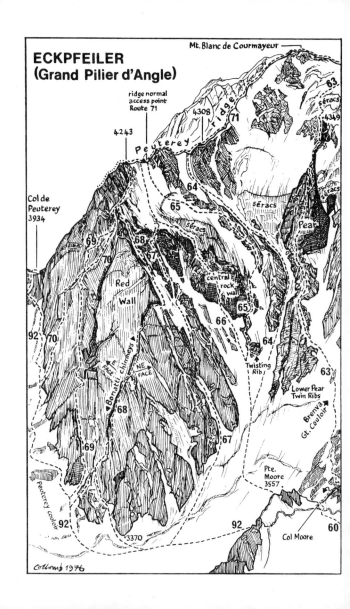

ECKPFEILER
(Grand Pilier d'Angle)

Mt. Blanc de Courmayeur

Peuterey ridge

Mt. Blanc de Courmayeur

63

séracs

4349

ridge normal
access point
Route 71

4308

71

4243

Peuterey ridge

64

Col de Peuterey
3934

65

séracs

séracs

séracs

Pear

69

68

67

central
rock
wall

66

65

64

Red
Wall

92

70

NE
FACE

Bonatti Chimneys

Twisting
Rib

63

Lower Pear
Twin Ribs

69

68

67

Brenva
Gt. Couloir

Pte.
Moore
3557

Peuterey couloir

92

92

92

Col Moore

60

3370

Collomb 1976

The first ascensionists and other parties exited L, under the sérac barrier by a couloir formation (very exposed to falling ice), and either went up direct to Mt. Blanc de Courmayeur or climbed R-wards through a breach in the barrier. Several ice pitches.

A relatively safe exit has been made L to the latter summit by leaving the direct ascent line just above the second couloir traverse (i.e. above Pointe Ultime), and climbing towards the Peuterey ridge by steep snow/ice, rocks and the crest of a buttress (IV), finishing L of the summit.

Conditions as to features encountered and degree of objective danger vary greatly for all exits. From Col Moore to summit ridge (10-14 h.).

Eckpfeiler Buttress or Grand Pilier d'Angle

Eckpfeiler, per Paul Güssfeldt, c. 1890. Frenchified in the 1930s. The summit of this great buttress rising out of the Brenva glacier at the L side of the Brenva face is pt. 4243 on the Peuterey ridge of Mt. Blanc. All of its routes are long and serious, and represent some of the most demanding climbs of their kind in the Alps. On reaching the top it is normal to continue to Mt. Blanc by the Peuterey ridge, which after an ascent of the buttress most parties have found long and tiring. Allow 5-8 h. to the top of Mt. Blanc. Alternatively the ridge can be descended to Col Peuterey followed by a descent of the Rochers Gruber to reach the Frêney glacier and the Monzino hut (6-8 h.). The climbs are described from R to L.

The best approach is from the Trident/Fourche/Brenva biv. huts across Col Moore, as for Route 60 (45 min. - 1¾ h. according to hut). From the col go up the initial snow ridge for a short way, then turn off L and descend steep snow under the lowest rocks and over a bergschrund into the S bay of the upper Brenva glacier. From here a short nearly horizontal traverse on snow (falling rocks and ice from above) leads towards the foot of the buttress (1-2 h.).

64 <u>North-East Face (Japanese Route)</u>. This most recent complete route up the R side of the face is also the most dangerous. It lies to the R of the Bonatti/Zappelli route and is threatened directly by the Pear séracs then by the Eckpfeiler

séracs. ED. It takes steep ice couloirs trending R then re-
sumes a direct ascent on ice. S. Inoue and S. Matsumi, on
the night of 29 July, 1974.

<u>North-East Face (Bonatti/Zappelli)</u>. A very serious and
and committing climb, unrepeated from 1962 to 1975. All
kinds of climbing but mostly hard work on ice with considerable
objective danger. Numerous rock and ice pegs required. ED.
650m. Considered inferior in quality to the Cecchinel/Nominé
route. First ascent: Walter Bonatti and C. Zappelli, 22-23
June, 1962. Second ascent (British): P. Braithwaite and
A. McIntyre; A. and A. Burgess, July, 1975. Solo ascent in
6 h. at night with major variations due to errors in route
finding by John Bouchard (American), July, 1975. Solo on
route: B. Macho, 4 August, 1975. At least two other ascents
in 1975. Winter: R. Chère and D. Monaci, 22-24 Dec.,1975.

65 From Col Moore it is better to follow the traverse line
used by Route 63 and approach the rocks at the base of the
Pear buttress. Keep on a lower line across the snow/ice
slopes of the Great Couloir in the Brenva face and pass below
the second bergschrund under the twin ribs terminating the
Pear rocks (2 h. from Col Moore).

Cross the second bergschrund L of a pt. below the Pear
rocks (falling ice) and climb the steep snow/ice slope above
which is runnelled and broken by old avalanches, and cut by
crevasses. This big slope is threatened by falling ice from
hanging glaciers between the Pear (R) and Eckpfeiler (L).
Trend L in the fall line of the hanging glacier above the top of
this side of the Eckpfeiler and by several ice pitches come up
alongside a twisting rock rib on your R, projecting into the
slope. Climb the rib for 150m. (III) to the foot of a large icy
rock wall. Traverse 30m. R below the wall to a pt. where it
is relatively low, then ascend direct in an icy groove line

(crux) for 120m. Exit R by an exposed and delicate traverse of 40m. across the base of the ice couloir running up R of the hanging glacier. On the far R side mount the bordering rock rib for about 300m., to the level of the ice cliffs of the hanging glacier opposite. Now slant diagonally L for 80m. across a steep ice scoop to reach the snow cap of the hanging glacier. Continue in the centre of steep snow/ice slopes to a final bergschrund and an ice slope rising to the narrow shoulder behind pt. 4243 on the Peuterey ridge (18 h. from initial bergschrund on first ascent, 12-14 h. subsequently).

66 North-East Face (Dufour/Fréhel). A line diverging from the Bonatti/Zappelli beside the lower twisting rib. From here it keeps L on steep ice and ascends the icy central rock wall further L and near its orographical centre to finish by a rising traverse L on ice under the sérac barrier. Above this the route corresponds with the final slope of the Cecchinel/Nominé route. Considerable objective danger and comparable with the Bonatti/Zappelli route. ED, $10\frac{1}{2}$ h. on first ascent: G. Dufour and J. Fréhel, 11 August, 1973. Repeated in 1975.

North-East Face (Cecchinel/Nominé). Easily the best and safest route on the face, giving fine steep climbing with equal interest on rock and very steep ice. Some danger from falling ice at the bottom, but once established on the route the risks are minimal. The route follows ice gullies L of the sérac fall line high on the face. The lower half is marked by an obvious and fairly straight couloir cutting the rockface, immediately down to the L of the big slope taken by the Bonatti/Zappelli route. ED-with pitches of V/V+ and A2. 750m. A good selection of rock and ice climbing equipment is needed. First ascent: W. Cecchinel and G. Nominé, 16-17 September, 1971. First British (third) ascent: R. Renshaw and J. Tasker, 3 September, 1973. In winter: H.-P. Kasper, I. Ganahl,

T. Holdener and R. Homberger, 22-23 December, 1974. Climbed about 15 times to end of 1975.

67 From near the base of the Eckpfeiler cross a big bergschrund or turn it on the R, and go up snow towards the steeply slanting base of the buttress. Cross another bergschrund and climb ice immediately under the face to the last ice couloir opening in it, before the wide slope further R opens out under the séracs of the Eckpfeiler and Pear buttress. Climb this couloir with increasing steepness (55°) until it narrows and is almost strangled. Take an overhanging groove on the R, normally very icy but variable (15m., V, A1/2, pegs), leading to a thin continuation couloir or runnel. The first pitch in this is normally on ice at 70° and requires étriers at the top (20m.). The next pitches are at 50-60°, then the couloir broadens to an icefield. About the level where the Bonatti/Gobbi route emerges on to the opposite L edge of this icefield, a break line appears in the rock spur to the R. Follow a diagonal ramp on snow/ice then rocks to the R, to near the edge of another smaller icefield further R. Trend L up a steep delicate slab to below a 15m. tower. Climb this on the L by a short icy crack then chimney, with an alternative overhanging entry movement from the R into the chimney portion (V+, pegs). Above, trend R then go up the crest line directly with moves to the R (awkward cracks, V, IV, V, sustained for 50m.). From a pt. with pegs and old slings in place make a pendulum abseil R for 10m. on to a block. Continue by a diagonal traverse R along a chimney/flake line for 40m. to the head of the rock barrier. Follow mixed ground above to the snow/ice slope flanking the L side of the hanging glacier, and go up this to the sharp snow saddle just below pt. 4243 on the Peuterey ridge (9-14 h. from last bergschrund below entry couloir).

<u>East Face (Bonatti/Gobbi)</u>. A serious expedition on all kinds of terrain with some danger from stonefall. The bed of the

main chimneys gives steep sustained climbing with much loose rock in the lower and middle sections. The chimneys form an obvious line cutting diagonally R across the lower part of the buttress up to an edge dividing the E and NE faces. A diversion on to the icy NE face leads back to the edge which is then followed to the top. On this upper part the best line is variable and not always obvious. Variations made somewhat further R are on very steep, mixed and icy ground. Numerous good bivouac sites. TD+ in good conditions, pitches of V and V+ inclusive of peg movements. 875m. First ascent: Walter Bonatti and Toni Gobbi, 1-3 August, 1957. First winter ascent: A. Dvorak, J. Kurczak, A. Mroz and T. Pietrowsky, 5-9 March, 1971. First British ascent: R. Lake and A. Dewison, 13 September, 1971. First solo: N. Jaeger, 1975 in 6 h. Climbed about 20 times to end of 1975.

68 At the base of the Eckpfeiler (3370m.), sometimes a bad roture, climb from the lowest pt. up a groove bending L for several pitches before easier rocks trend R to the base of the obvious chimney line. Alternatively, go up steep snow under the buttress towards the Col de Peuterey, to a pt. directly below the chimney line. Cross a bergschrund and climb straightforward rocks to the foot of the chimneys.

The first steep and loose section (V+, A1) can be mainly avoided by a circuit to the R. First climb a pitch trending L (IV), then traverse R (V) to loose easy ground leading R below a steep wall. At the far end enter a hidden groove and go up this past a large overhang to an obvious stance (30m., V+). Step R and climb smooth rock into a couloir leading back L (20m., V+). Follow the couloir to rejoin the chimney line (40m., V). From here the chimney beds are filled with loose blocks; the side walls are usually climbed, or ribs to L or R. Good stances and belays.

Climb the chimney with difficult constrictions to a wide portion taken on the R wall by a thin crack (V+) then on the rib. Continue trending R up mainly pitches of IV/IV+ to another difficult constriction partly climbed on the R up a shallow groove, to finish L (V+). Above this a wide chimney leads to a small terrace below the key rock pitch. From the top of a block climb a fine crack in a dièdre on the R for 25m. (V+ with several pegs), then trend L to a niche below an overhang. Climb the overhang (V+, wedge) to a narrow snowy terrace line running R. Traverse R over mixed ground and slightly downwards to a large loose chimney/couloir. Climb this (III/IV) and exit R by a crack (IV/IV+). Follow grooves (IV) to the corner at the edge of the NE face.

From here traverse R and somewhat downwards over icy mixed ground for c.50m. to below a vague shallow couloir line in the face. Climb this trending L for 3-4 pitches on smooth ice worn rocks (IV, delicate) and after 150m. work L as soon as possible by a system of cracks (IV) to rejoin the edge or ridge. The L-ward movement can be made from a lower pt., according to conditions. Continue up the ridge on good rock with pitches of II, III and IV to mixed ground and snow leading to the Peuterey ridge (13-20 h. from foot of buttress).

69 <u>East Face (Polish Route)</u>. This route starts up the buttress at a depression in the wall some 150m. up the couloir leading to the Col de Peuterey. It follows a line progressively L, and on approaching the Peuterey ridge returns R to finish at the top of the Eckpfeiler. A long and serious route with continuous artificial climbing in some sections. Stonefall hazard. ED, A2/A3. 250 pegs, 5 wedges and one bolt used on first ascent: E. Chrobak, T. Laukajtys and A. Mroz, 15-20 July, 1969.

70 <u>East-South-East Face</u>. A facet of the Eckpfeiler which is started from a pt. about 300m. up the couloir of the Col de

Peuterey. A fine rock climb, crossing the upper part of the Polish route; its finish corresponds to the latter. TD with pitches of V+. First ascent: Walter Bonatti and C. Zappelli, 11-12 October, 1963. First winter ascent: A. and G. Rusconi, February, 1975.

———

Peuterey Ridge. This tremendous ridge rises from the Col de Peuterey (3934m.), which is not a pt. normally gained directly by its flanks, i. e. from the Brenva or Frêney glaciers, although in modern times the col has been reached thus for this and other purposes on numerous occasions. The ascent of the ridge to Mt. Blanc is normally preceded by a traverse of the Aig. Blanche from the Brèche des Dames Anglaises. This is the classic method of climbing the Peuterey ridge, making one of the longest and finest routes of its class in the Alps. The climbing is nowhere technically difficult, nor is the route finding particularly tricky, but the length combined with the inherent hazard of falling stones and the dangers of bad weather make it a serious undertaking. D+, variable according to snow conditions.

The expedition can be split by a bivouac either at the Brèche N des Dames Anglaises biv. hut, or on the lower rocks of Pte. Gugliermina. This is the most comfortable method unless the snow conditions were good and the party fit which would enable them to reach the Vallot hut from the Monzino in a day. The best bad weather descent is by the Rochers Gruber from the Col de Peuterey, q. v. This part of Mt. Blanc is particularly susceptible to storms and great care must be taken to avoid being trapped on the ridge.

First ascent: L. Obersteiner and K. Schreiner, 30-31 July, 1927. First British ascent: T. Graham Brown with A. Graven and J. Knubel, 30 July, 1932. First solo: Richard Hechtel,

1937. Record ascent from Gamba (Monzino) hut to summit of Mt. Blanc in 10 h. by R. V. M. Barry with Armand Charlet in 1936.

Many combinations are possible for climbing the Peuterey ridge over the Aig. Blanche. The most ambitious of these, again variable, is to traverse firstly the Aig. Noire. This is known as the Peuterey "Integral". The easiest start is by the normal E ridge of the Noire, but the complete traverse has been done on several occasions by parties starting up the famous S ridge of the Noire (also by even harder routes on its W face). These combinations add up to the longest and one of the most difficult traverses of its kind in the Alps. Probably the best way of doing it is to leave a cache of food on the summit of the Noire or at the biv. hut on the Brèche N des Dames Anglaises.

First integral ascent (by E ridge of Noire): A. Goettner, L. Schmaderer and F. Krobath, 28-31 July, 1934. By S ridge of Noire: R. Hechtel and G. Kittelmann, 24-26 July, 1953. In winter by S ridge: M. Feuillarade, Y. Seigneur, L. Audoubert, M. Galy, A. and O. Squinobal, 22-26 December, 1972. First solo by S ridge: René Desmaison, 10-12 August, 1972.

71 From the Monzino hut follow Route 18 to the foot of the couloir leading to the Brèche N des Dames Anglaises. From here there are two alternatives:

(i) Continue by Route 18 directly up the couloir to the biv. hut on the Brèche Nord.

(ii) About 150m. L of the foot of the couloir is a long diagonal shallow couloir, crossing the lower rocks of the Pte. Gugliermina and leading up to the SE ridge of the Aig. Blanche. Start below the couloir, just R of a rock rognon in the glacier. An overhung gangway (good biv. site) leads R to a chimney. Climb this (III) into the couloir proper (Schneider couloir) and follow the bed, sometimes snow, to a short distance below the SE ridge. On your R are the last two gendarmes on a subsidiary ridge before the latter joins the main SE ridge above. Move R and pass between these, and descend a short steep couloir to a descending traverse line leading down a short chimney and continuing to traverse L (E) to the Brèche Nord. This descent is only necessary to reach the biv. hut.

From the Brèche Nord traverse horizontally L on bad rock to the foot of a short chimney. Climb this then follow a ledge line L for 40m. into a small slabby couloir leading to a notch in the subsidiary ridge. This notch is the one between the two gendarmes at the start of the corresponding descent described above. From the notch climb a short secondary couloir on the R of the subsidiary ridge which leads to easy rocks and so to the main SE ridge of the Aig. Blanche, at the top of the steep buttress which dominates the Brèche Nord. Follow the ridge for a minute, then traverse on to the Brenva side of the Pte. Gugliermina. Keep in a horizontal line at first, on easy broken slabs, then trend up diagonally R across broken rocky crests, separated by shallow couloirs, until a secondary ridge, about the third, leads back to the main ridge, just before a circular rocky gap about a third of the distance from Pte. Gugliermina to the summit of the Aig. Blanche. Climb the ridge and descend keeping R to the gap. Continue up the ridge with short pitches of II, keeping slightly on the Frêney side, until snow is reached. Go straight up the snow to the summit of the SE Pte. of the Aig. Blanche (4107m.) (3-6 h. from the Brèche Nord).

Descend a short chimney of bad rock to the thin and airy snow crest running to the Central summit. Cross this (large cornices) and pass below the Central summit (4122m.) on the Brenva side. Continue along the ridge, then traverse the flank of the snowy rocks of the NW summit (4104m.). A short distance along the crest is a small biv. site on the Frêney side (1-2 h. on average for summit ridge). Now descend diagonally towards the Col de Peuterey in steep loose gullies on the

Frêney side, go over a bergschrund and down a steep snow/ice slope to the snowy plateau of the Col de Peuterey (3934m.). In poor conditions, make three abseils in and alongside the gullies, and another over and below the bergschrund. Two ropes of at least 40m. are most useful (average time for this descent, 2 h., but it can take considerably longer).

From the Col de Peuterey there are two alternatives to reach the top of the Eckpfeiler buttress (4243m.).

(i) The most elegant and least exposed to stonefall. Keeping L of the crest, traverse diagonally L up the snow or ice for about 60m., to the pt. where the angle of the rocks above becomes easier. The bergschrund here may be difficult. Cross it and climb to the rocks above, and follow these slanting R to the ridge crest. Go up the ridge more or less directly and without special difficulty to the shoulder of the Eckpfeiler and continue along this by a fine snow crest, passing a large gendarme on the Brenva side ($2\frac{1}{2}$-$4\frac{1}{2}$ h.).

(ii) The quicker if the snow is in good condition. Traverse diagonally L as for (i), but keep below the rocks until directly below the large gendarme on the shoulder of the Eckpfeiler, about 150m. distance from the col. Cross the bergschrund (often awkward) and climb a snow/ice slope to snowy rocks (stonefall) which in turn are climbed to the shoulder either L or R of the gendarme (2-4 h.).

After the gendarme go up a ridge step keeping R then follow the rocky ridge which rises gently to the long snow ridge leading to Mt. Blanc de Courmayeur. This ridge is often icy, and is rarely completely free of ice. Relief may be found by climbing small rock buttresses which occur at intervals on either side of the ridge. The exit is usually guarded by a cornice, which provides a final obstacle. Continue on easy snow slopes above to the summit of Mt. Blanc de Courmayeur (2-8 h.).

Traverse the ridge to the NW, contouring some rocks on

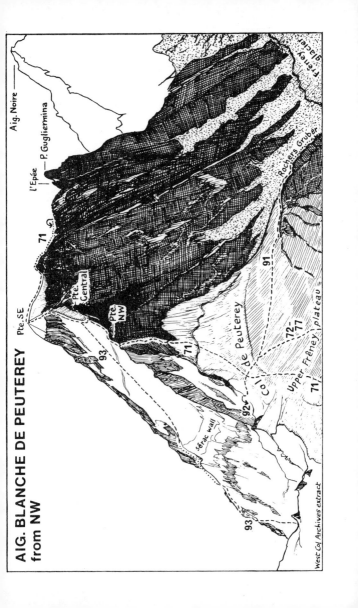

AIG. BLANCHE DE PEUTEREY
from NW

Aig. Noire

P. Gugliermina

l'Epée

Pte. SE

Pte. Central

Pte. NW

71

71

93

93

92

92

91

72·
77

71

Col de Peuterey

Upper Frêney plateau

Rochers Gruber

Frêney glacier

sérac wall

West Col Archives extract

the L, to the summit of Mt. Blanc (5-11 h. from Col de
Peuterey; 6-15 h. from the Aig. Blanche; 13-27 h. from
Monzino hut).

Frêney Face

The E face of Mt. Blanc de Courmayeur is formed between
the Peuterey ridge (N) and the Innominata ridge (S) as the
headwall of a steep ice cwm and narrow plateau above the
Frêney glacier. The face is divided into two parts by a large
snow couloir descending from just below pt. 4704 on the upper
part of the Brouillard ridge. To the R of this couloir is the
Direct Route to Mt. Blanc de Courmayeur; to the L are four
huge granite pillars rising for 700m. from the upper Frêney
plateau towards the Brouillard ridge.
    The pillars (coined thus by G. Gervasutti, c.1938) give
some of the finest and hardest climbing on Mt. Blanc, in
remote and wild surroundings. The approach to them is long
and serious - an expedition in itself. The seriousness of
retreat in bad weather cannot be emphasised too strongly,
since the fastest descent, by the Rochers Gruber, is exposed
to stonefall and involves crossing the very crevassed Frêney
glacier.
    There are several approaches to the upper Frêney plateau.
The Peuterey couloir seems the most popular and is probably
the fastest route.

Approaches to upper Frêney plateau

(a) From the Monzino hut to the Eccles biv. hut, see Route 17
(5-7 h.). PD. From here climb loose rocks and snow R-wards
to the SW spur of Pic Eccles and follow the steep crest line,
keeping R, to Pic Eccles (4041m.). Alternatively stop just
below the top of Pic Eccles, turn the summit on the L side and
join snow running into the depression of Col Eccles (c. 4000m.).
Either way, AD-. Continue along the short snow ridge to the
N end, at the foot of the first step on the Innominata ridge
($1\frac{3}{4}$ h.). Now descend diagonally L (looking out) on broken
rocks under the latter step to reach the steep snow/ice slope
above the bergschrund at this end of the upper Frêney plateau.
Descend this slope and cross the bergschrund (often difficult)
to continue across the sloping plateau (AD+) (1-2 h., $2\frac{3}{4}$-$3\frac{3}{4}$ h.

from Eccles biv. hut).

(b) From the Monzino hut by the Frêney glacier (variable approach) and the Rochers Gruber. See under Col de Peuterey. Generally speaking not recommended in view of the tedious section on the lower Frêney glacier. AD/AD+ (6-8 h. from hut to plateau).

(c) From the Trident or Fourche huts. As for the E side couloir of the Col de Peuterey (q.v.). From the col make a slightly descending traverse for some distance on snow to the sloping plateau. D (5-8 h.).

72 Direct Route. A fine mountaineering route on mixed terrain, taking the Great Couloir for about 250m. then breaking out R to follow a direct line to Mt. Blanc de Courmayeur. TD- with a section of V. First ascent: Walter Bonatti and C. Zappelli, 21 September, 1961 (11 h.). Second ascent (solo): B. Macho, 4 August, 1975. Winter ascent by 3 Japanese, 18-23 Jan. 1976.

73 Frêney Great Couloir. Mainly a snow/ice climb with a notable rock section on thin snow/ice bands, comparable with the Peuterey couloir but somewhat longer. Stonefall danger throughout though minimal in good conditions. D+ with pitches of IV. First ascent: G. Abert, M. Afanassieff, J. Blanchard and O. Challéat, 30 July, 1974.

Frêney Right-Hand (Gervasutti) Pillar. The fairly broken pillar containing the L side of the Great Couloir. A fine climb on rock, ice and mixed terrain. The rock is fairly sound with one bad section. There is little objective danger. Climbed infrequently, so few pegs will be found in place. TD and A1, with pitches of V, V+ and VI. First ascent: P. Bollini and G. Gervasutti, 13 August, 1940. First British ascent: G. Francis and G. J. Sutton with Lionel Terray, 31 July, 1952.

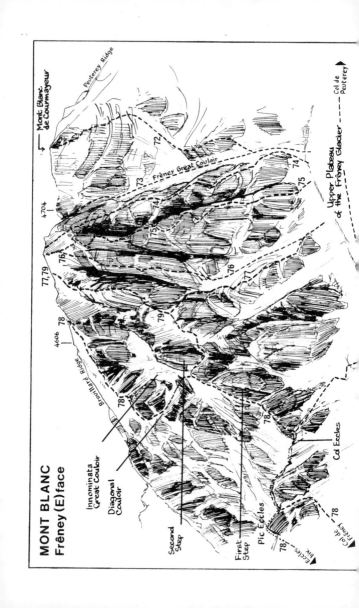

MONT BLANC
Frêney (E) face

Mont Blanc
de Courmayeur

Peuterey Ridge

Col de
Peuterey

4.704

Frêney Great Couloir

Upper Plateau
of the Frêney Glacier

Brouillard Ridge

4.606

Innominata
Great Couloir

Diagonal
Couloir

Second
Step

First
Step

Pic Eccles

Col Eccles

Eccles
bivi.

Col de
Frêney

72
73
74
75
75
76
76
77
77,79
78
78
79
78
78
78
78
78
78

First solo: P. Béghin, 21 August, 1973. First winter ascent: J. Coudray, C. Daubas and R. Renaud, 24-28 January, 1974. Probably climbed 10 times to end of 1975.

74 From the upper Fréney plateau cross the bergschrund in a line L of the pillar, then traverse diagonally R on steep snow/ice to the R-hand base of the rocks. Climb easy rocks to the foot of the first step. Now traverse R to the edge of the Great Couloir and go up this on loose snowy rocks (III) till a curving groove on the L can soon be climbed (IV) to the top of the step. A short ice slope leads to a deep gap, crossed by a very thin snow/ice crest, to reach the second step. One pitch leads to the foot of a 40m. grey slab split by two cracks. Climb the R-hand one which trends R to the ridge on that side (VI, A1, several pegs). Follow a ledge line R and at its end climb a very loose red wall, trending L for 30m. to below a small overhang (III+). Now traverse R (V+, strenuous) to a small niche. Above this go up a small overhang (V) into a well defined narrow chimney. Climb it, often icy (V) and continue on the R side of the ridge for 20m. Avoid the next step by working L into a parallel couloir depression. Ascend this, icy with snow patches and smooth rock pitches, keeping L at first then climbing on the R side (III/IV). Keep L at the top and exit L onto the broken upper slopes. Cross these diagonally L to the corniced Brouillard ridge (11-14 h. from bergschrund to ridge).

Fréney Central Pillar. One of the finest and hardest climbs on Mt. Blanc, combining the general mountaineering difficulties of the approach with some high standard rock climbing above 4000m. TD+ with a section of VI, or V+ and A1 with sufficient pegs in place. Many of the fine free pitches suffer from over-pegging. In particular the Chandelle may be found completely artificial below the roof. Most parties bivouac once below the Chandelle. First ascent: C. J. S. Bonington, I. S. Clough,

111

D. D. Whillans and J. Djuglosz, 27-29 August, 1961. A party led by René Desmaison followed immediately behind the British party. First winter ascent: R. Desmaison and R. Flematty, 1-6 February, 1967. Solo ascent: G. Nominé, 8-9 September, 1971. Climbed about 40 times to end of 1975.

75 From the upper Frêney plateau climb to the foot of the pillar, below an obvious groove. To the R some cracks and ledges give a line of weakness. Climb diagonally R for 30m. (III) over slabs to the foot of a chimney and go up this (V) to its top. Continue for two pitches, first to the L and then on the R, up short walls and snow patches (III) to reach the foot of a groove in the centre of the face. Climb a slab on its R for 30m. (V) to a ledge below a corner topped by a roof. Move up R to another groove and follow this to a line of overhangs. Traverse L back on to the face of the pillar (V). Follow a crack on the L (IV) then go back up to the R to a snow shoulder on the crest of the pillar. Continue up cracks to the foot of a slab and up a crack in its corner (IV), to the foot of a sharp rib. Climb a slab and snow patches, then go diagonally L to the foot of a chimney. Climb the chimney for 20m. (V+), then up to the shoulder below where the pillar becomes steeper and very smooth. Traverse over snow to the foot of a semi-detached pedestal.

Climb the crack L of the pedestal to its top (15m., A1, V). Bivouac site. Above, climb cracks to the overhang at 20m. (A1, V). Traverse R beneath the overhang for 8m. (originally A2, VI) and step down to a small hold and peg belay in a shallow niche near the edge of the pillar. Traverse 12m. R, round the corner, on to the R wall of the pillar (VI or A1) to the foot of a groove topped by a large roof. Climb the groove (small wooden wedges in place, V+ or A2) for 20m., then go up to the chimney going through the roof (A2). Climb the cracked wall above to a ledge going across the face of the pillar (V).

112

Follow the ledge to the L-hand side of the pillar. Bivouac site on a ledge 9m. below, on the SW face. Climb cracks near the SW edge of the pillar for 30m. (IV), then take a slab for 30m. (V) to the top of the pillar. A short abseil leads to a small col behind (bivouac sites), from where snow/ice slopes and mixed terrain lead to the Brouillard ridge (average recent time from upper plateau to ridge, 13 h.; another 2-3 h. up ridge to Mt. Blanc).

76 Hidden Pillar. In sideways views it is largely concealed to the L of the Central Pillar. A difficult climb at high altitude in a serious position on perfect rock. TD+ with pitches of VI and A3. First ascent: T. Frost and J. Harlin, 1-2 August, 1963. Second ascent: S. Belak and B. Krivic, 18-19 July, 1969.

77 Frêney South Pillar. More of a mountaineering route and probably the easiest of the Frêney pillars. Mixed climbing, TD- with pitches of V, V+ and A1. First ascent: L. Dubost and Y. Seigneur, 25-26 July, 1972. First winter ascent: G. Decorps, G. Gaby and R. Mizrahi, January, 1976.

Innominata Ridge. The somewhat complicated but quite definite ridge dividing the Frêney and Brouillard faces of Mt. Blanc. The climb proper starts at Col Eccles. Below this it is the massive Innominata ridge which divides the Frêney and Brouillard glaciers, down to the Monzino hut. One of the best of the classic routes up Mt. Blanc, slightly more difficult but shorter than the Peuterey ridge. D with pitches of III and IV. Above Col Eccles the route is very steep and the rock is excellent. The great couloir section is subject to stonefall. Normally one starts from the Eccles biv. hut, but in good conditions and with an early start, it is feasible to reach the Vallot hut from the Monzino hut in one day. The time record for this ascent is constantly being broken. First ascent:

S. L. Courtauld and E. G. Oliver with A. Aufdenblatten and A. and H. Rey, 19-20 August, 1919. First winter ascent: G. Panei and S. Viotto, 25 March, 1953. Solo ascent: L. Audoubert, 28 August, 1973 (Monzino hut to summit of Mt. Blanc in 8 h.).

78 From the Monzino hut to Eccles biv. hut, see Route 17. From here climb loose rocks and snow R-wards to the SW spur of Pic Eccles and follow the steep crest line, keeping R, to Pic Eccles (4041m.). Alternatively stop just below the top of Pic Eccles, turn the summit on the L side and join snow running into the depression of Col Eccles (c. 4000m.). Either way, AD-. When climbing direct from the Monzino hut, a slightly quicker way to reach Col Eccles from Col Frêney (Route 17) would be to follow the long steeply shelving snow slope band which runs diagonally above the Frêney precipices. This leads to a short, steep and narrow gully which reaches the ridge near Pic Eccles. AD.

Follow the sharp horizontal snow crest of Col Eccles to the foot of the first steep rock step. Do not attempt to avoid this on the L. Climb the ridge itself by very steep pitches on good rock (III), keeping a little on the L side, to the foot of two red towers. Climb a chimney which leads to a narrow ledge at the foot of a short steep wall, to the R of the first tower. Climb this wall by a little crack (IV, 6m.), turn the tower on the R and continue up to a hole, which forms the col behind the tower. Leaving the second tower on the L, climb a steep crest on good holds (III).

Follow a short, narrow, horizontal snow crest to the foot of the second step, which consists of huge red columns of granite. Trend L up among steep rocks towards the great ice couloir, which separates the ridge from a secondary buttress more to the W. The couloir is reached at a point where it steepens abruptly, and passes between wet slabs. Just above this pt. traverse across the couloir for 30m. (stonefall) to the first bit of rock sticking out of the ice. Leave this almost immediately, moving further L to a second group of rocks. Climb these easily to a narrow ice couloir slanting to the L, at the foot of a steep red tower. Climb the steep couloir to reach the crest of the rock buttress, which defines the L side of the region around the great couloir.

Follow this buttress, keeping near the crest and slightly on its L side. It consists of a series of rock steps separated by short ice slopes or snow ridges, sometimes corniced. It ends in a steep snow ridge about 150m. high, which merges with the main ridge. Continue up the ridge, or the ice slope on its L to reach the crest of the Brouillard ridge, which is followed to the summit of Mt. Blanc (8-11 h. from the Eccles biv.).

Variation on the Innominata Ridge, by the Frêney Face. Less logical than the classical route, but nevertheless a nice climb. The difficulties are more in keeping with the lower part of the ridge, giving a more continuous climb. It ascends the top part of the L-hand (South) Frêney Pillar. D. First ascent: T. Graham Brown with Alexander Graven and Alfred Aufdenblatten, 9 August, 1933.

79 Follow Route 78 to the foot of the second step. From this pt. make a descending traverse R, under the wall of the step. This leads to a small rock couloir. Cross this, climb a ridge for a short way, and cross a second couloir. Continue to the R over snow and rocks, to the ridge situated immediately R of the true Innominata Ridge (this pt. can also be reached by a descending traverse from the top of the second step). Climb this ridge till it steepens and narrows into a very steep step. Climb this by gullies, chimneys and cracks (III and IV). Above the step, follow the crest of the ridge to the terminal snow slopes, which lead to the Brouillard ridge (9-12 h. from the Eccles biv. to top of Mt. Blanc).

MONT BLANC SE side

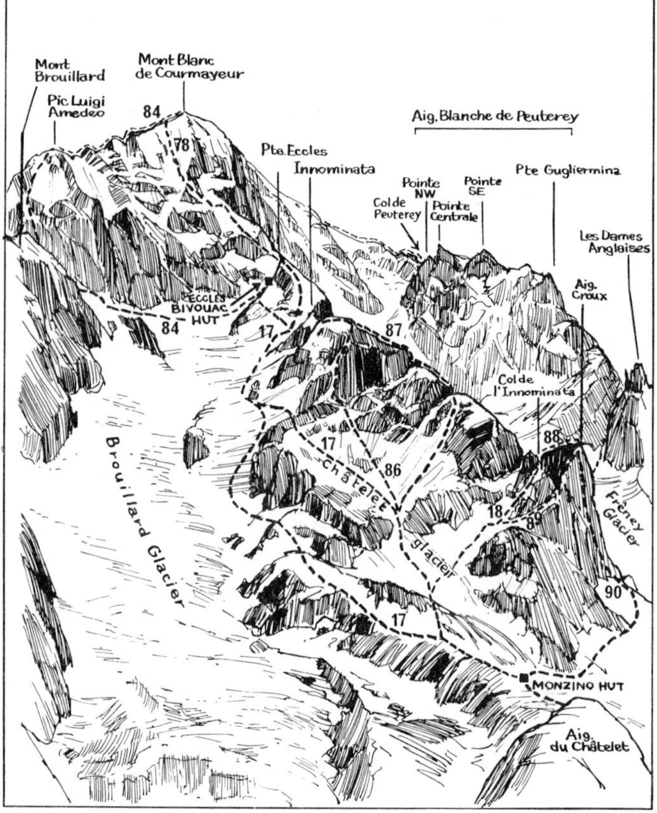

Mont Brouillard

Pic Luigi Amedeo

Mont Blanc de Courmayeur

84

78

Pte. Eccles Innominata

Aig. Blanche de Peuterey

Pointe NW

Pointe SE

Pte Gugliermina

Col de Peuterey

Pointe Centrale

Les Dames Anglaises

Aig. Croux

ECCLES BIVOUAC HUT

84

17

87

Col de l'Innominata

88

17

Châtelet

86

18

8

Brouillard Glacier

glacier

Fréney Glacier

90

17

MONZINO HUT

Aig. du Châtelet

Brouillard Face

Situated L (SW) of the Innominata ridge and forming a SE face under the Brouillard ridge, about the middle part of which in this lower section is found P. Luigi Amedeo (4460m.). Conspicuous in the lower part of the face at the head of the Brouillard glacier it is possible to distinguish four pillars of red granite, rising for about half the height of 600m. to the ridge. The lower section of these pillars is very steep and gives superb climbing on perfect rock.

As with the Frêney pillars, the approaches are long and difficult and retreat in bad weather can be arduous and dangerous. The Brouillard glacier is extremely crevassed, and in some years may be completely impassable, particularly late in the season when the crevasses are more open.

Brouillard Right-Hand Pillar.

Superb climbing on perfect rock, taking a direct line up the crest of the pillar, TD+ and A2 with a pitch of VI. The pillar section is 300m. Probably the most reasonable of the great rock routes on the S side of Mt. Blanc, with only short sections of artificial climbing. The best approach is from the Eccles biv., which avoids the principal difficulties of the glacier. First ascent: C. J. S. Bonington and J. Harlin; R. W. Baillie and B. Robertson, 21 August, 1965, to the Brouillard ridge. Second ascent: R. Everett and L. Griffin, 1973.

80 From the Eccles biv. hut, traverse horizontally over steep mixed terrain for two rope lengths, then descend a short pitch on snow/ice to the upper part of the Brouillard glacier, to reach a tongue of snow leading up to the foot of the R-hand pillar.

Trend slightly R up a series of grooves, towards the couloir on the R of the pillar, for 20m. to a niche topped by a square-cut roof (IV). Step L just below the niche (peg) into a crack and go up this (V) to some good ledges where the angle eases. Step L and go up into a shallow flake chimney, which leads back R into the couloir on the R of the pillar (V). Follow the gully up snow for a few m., until it is possible to return to some broken ledges. Climb the short strenuous groove above (V) to a narrow ledge, then make an airy traverse L (IV+) round the corner and follow easy rocks into the centre of the face.

Climb broken rocks (III and IV) to the foot of a diagonal groove, which leads up to the highest ledge visible on the crest of the pillar. From the ledge, climb the open corner on the R of the crest (A2 and VI) to a wide ledge. A groove slants back to the L (IV+) to the foot of the single crack which splits the compact upper face of the pillar.

Climb the crack (A1 and V+, 8 pegs) for 30m., to just below a small overhang. Stance in étriers. Climb under the overhang (V+)   and go over it to a peg in place. From the peg, tension down to the R across the slab to two shallow parallel cracks. Climb these to a ledge on the edge of the pillar. Climb the open corner on the L (A1, 2 pegs) then traverse diagonally L (IV+) towards a pinnacle on the skyline, until it is possible to climb straight up to the crest of the pillar by some cracks (V). Climb easy slabs diagonally L (III) to the top R-hand end of a short steep wall. Climb this (V+, one peg) to the end of the steep section of the pillar.

Above, the pillar leans back and becomes broader. Follow a crest of snow patches and loose rock, trending L all the way to reach the Brouillard ridge a little R of P. Luigi Amedeo (10-14 h. from Eccles biv. to ridge).

<u>Brouillard Central Pillar</u>. The main part of the pillar has been climbed by two distinct lines, that on the R edge being quite obvious. This is the route described below. The principal difficulties amount to 400m., giving excellent climbing on superb granite. TD+ and A1 with pitches of V+. There is stonefall danger throughout and there seems to be no sheltered bivouac places. First ascent: Eric Jones, solo, 15-16 July, 1971, to the Brouillard ridge. On reaching the ridge he was

caught by a storm and was rescued two days later by helicopter.

81 From the Eccles biv. start as for the previous route. From the upper Brouillard glacier cross a large bergschrund below the pillar and ascend steep snow/ice to its base. Start at an obvious line to the L of a grey section. Climb for 150m. (IV) with two icy chimneys (V). When level with a large capstone climb for 50m. then traverse R to the bottom of two dièdres. Climb the L one for 50m. (V, V+), then go up broken steps to another dièdre. Climb this for 40m. then traverse R across an icy gully to a ledge (IV). Follow this to its end. Abseil 10m. to another ledge, bivouac site. From here traverse R into a crack and climb it until it overhangs (IV). Move R on to a pinnacle at the edge of the couloir separating the R-hand and Central pillars (serious stonefall danger). Step L off pinnacle into a crack line, climb a short overhang and the continuation crack (A1 and V+). From the top of the crack climb a small bulge and a blunt ridge to an expansion bolt. Tension L from the bolt to another crack and take this to the top of the pillar (IV). From the top climb mixed ground for 270m. to the Brouillard ridge (14 h. climbing time).

<u>Red Pillar.</u> The more obvious L-hand pillar on the face, a well defined tower of superb red rock, giving a splendid free and mixed climb at high altitude. The pillar itself is about 350m. The base of it is exposed to stonefall and it is essential to reach the rocks as early as possible. ED-, pitches of V, V+ and VI (A1). In 16 pitches only 3 are IV, the rest harder, and the climbing is nearly always strenuous. First ascent: Walter Bonatti and A. Oggioni, 5-6 July, 1960. First British (second) ascent, by Var. Start: A. Burgess and R. Shaw, 13-14 July, 1971 (in 9 h. to ridge). First winter ascent: R. Ito and N. Ogawa, 21-23 January, 1972.

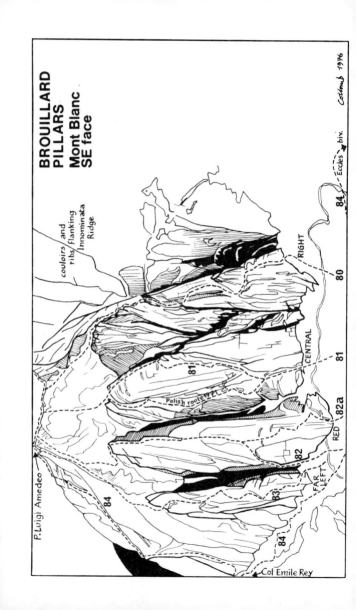

BROUILLARD
PILLARS
Mont Blanc
SE face

couloirs and ribs flanking Innominata Ridge

P.Luigi Amedeo

Polish route 1971

RIGHT

CENTRAL

RED

FAR LEFT

Col Emile Rey

Eccles biv.

Coldwb 1976

84 80 81 82a 82 83 84

82 From the Eccles biv. hut start as for Route 80 and cross the Brouillard glacier to below the pillar. Start up the icy gully L of the pillar and ascend for 40m. (great danger from stonefall), then traverse diagonally R on broken icy rocks to reach a system of terraces. Follow these round the corner on to the middle of the face (2-3 h.).

Take a system of steep cracks and compact slabs with few belay ledges (V, VI-, pegs) to reach the foot of a deep chimney in the centre of the face. The variation start joins here. Climb the chimney, sometimes icy, and exit R to a stance (30m., V+). Climb a slab and move L into a steepening groove. Follow this until it is possible to exit L into a loose icy gully. Ascend the gully for 15m. to a belay ledge on L, at the base of the upper tower. Steep slabs lead to an over-hanging crack line on the L. Take this to a tiny ledge below a bulging crack, and climb the latter (V+, peg). A steep icy crack is avoided by moving L under a roof, then return R to exit L on a sloping ledge. Follow a steep crack line to a slab belay. Continue up the corner, move L in cracks and go up a deep icy chimney (loose). Exit L at the top. Climb a corner and continue in obvious groove and cracks to the top. Descend to the small col behind the pillar (6-8 h.).

Continue up a broad broken ridge to the top of P. Luigi Amedeo on the lower part of the Brouillard ridge (3 h., 11-14 h. from below entry couloir to ridge).

82A Variation start, just R of the centre of the pillar base, joining the original route at the main chimneys in the middle of the face. ED, 35 pegs.

Start climbing at a pt. just R of centre, on steep slabs and snow, trending R. Return L on an easy terrace into the centre of the face. Take an obvious diagonal crack trending R (45m., IV+). Continue up to the L over snowy rocks till a traverse line leads L below the steep lower section of the pillar (45m.).

A steep crack is the only line of weakness. Climb this for 25m. to a large belay ledge (VI, loose, pegs), then climb trending L to the chimneys on the original route.

83 <u>Brouillard Far Left Pillar.</u> A remote and serious climb. ED- with pitches of VI and some poor rock. First ascent: R. Kowalewski, J. Maczka and W. Wroz, 13-14 August, 1971 (10 h. from bergschrund to Brouillard ridge).

<u>Brouillard Ridge (from Col Emile Rey).</u> One of the classic routes to Mt. Blanc, not as fine or as interesting as the Peuterey or the Innominata but as long and as variable as these ridges with the chief problem concerned with choice of approach to the ridge at Col Emile Rey (4030m.). Once above the col the lower rock and mixed sections up to and beyond P. Luigi Amedeo (4460m.) are mostly loose and can be dangerous unless conveniently frozen by just-right conditions which in terms of fresh snow or ice would not upgrade the general standard of climbing, which is normally less serious than the Peuterey and Innominata. The upper ridge is a superb high level snow crest, less demanding than the comparable section of the Peuterey. AD/AD+. Nearly all ascents today are made up the E side of Col Emile Rey from the Monzino or Eccles huts. In poor conditions there is considerable stonefall danger on the final ascent to the col and on the rocks above it up to P. Luigi Amedeo. Other approaches are ignored although the W side of Col Emile Rey is described in the next route. The Brouillard ridge was first climbed in 1901 by a direct ascent on the W flank of P. Luigi Amedeo, and complete from Col Emile Rey, also approached from the W side, by K. Blodig, H. O. Jones and G. W. Young with J. Knubel, 9 August, 1911. It was not climbed complete by an ascent from the E side (described below) until 1933, after which this route became quite popular. A solo ascent from the Monzino hut to summit

of Mt. Blanc was made by L. Audoubert on 26 July, 1970 in 6 h. In winter:J. Clémenson, B.&G. Dufour, 14-15 Jan,1976.

84 From the Monzino hut to Eccles biv., see Route 17 (5-7 h.). From the Eccles biv. traverse horizontally over steep mixed terrain for two rope lengths, then descend a short pitch on snow/ice to the upper terrace of the Brouillard glacier. Traverse the glacier under the Brouillard pillars (stonefall) and mount the bulging snow tongue running out of the couloir under the wall of P. Luigi Amedeo on the R. Cross a bergschrund on the L and climb steep snow to a short snow rib running up to the wall again. Work below the wall as far as possible. Steep snow/ice may then compel a traverse L to rocks in the centre of the terminal slope. It is debatable whether it is more sheltered here or under the wall. Climb the rocks as quickly as possible, trending R at the top to reach the fine snow crest of Col Emile Rey ($1\frac{1}{2}$-2 h.).

From the col get on to the E (R) side of P. Luigi Amedeo and work along and down for 20m. to the foot of a steep narrow rock gully cutting the S side of the mtn. Climb the gully, delicate in parts, avoiding a steep groove by a smooth flanking slab (10m., III). This section is exposed to stonefall. After three more rope lengths the gully opens out on to broken ground situated R of a gendarme. The ridge proper is still a long way above. Go up the rocks trending a little R for about 30 min. then take a long snow slope (stonefall) or a rib on its R for about 1 h. to the ridge. Follow the ridge over a jumble of blocks, not far, to the summit of P. Luigi Amedeo ($2\frac{1}{2}$-4 h.).

From the Amedeo summit descend the steep shattered ridge crest keeping somewhat R to the level of a gap in the ridge at this pt. From a few m. below the gap move R and climb a wall on the R side of the ridge to steep, loose but easier rocks leading to the top of the step above the gap. A corresponding longer wall pitch using a crack (III+) can be climbed from the gap on the L side of the ridge, which is better rock. Now follow a narrow horizontal section, then go over snow and steep pinnacled blocks to a second step somewhat less steep than the first. Climb this on the R side by moderate rocks and loose mixed terrain. Then a short horizontal section along a fine crest leads to a riser marking the approx. junction (4606m.) with the Innominata ridge. Continue along the mainly sharp and delicate snow crest, cornices possible, with short rock sections. Turn a 30m. rock step on its L side by steep mixed terrain. After this the L side of the ridge can be contoured on snow/ice below the summit of Mt. Blanc de Courmayeur to rejoin the easy ridge beyond, before the Tourette rocks, and after these rocks the calotte of Mt. Blanc itself is soon reached ($3\frac{1}{2}$-6 h., 6-10 h. from Col Emile Rey, $7\frac{1}{2}$-12 h. from Eccles biv.).

Brouillard · Innominata · Peuterey spurs

COL EMILE REY   4030m.   4027m. IGM

Between P. Luigi Amedeo and Mt. Brouillard. A superb col in wild surroundings. It is not a practised passage between the Brouillard and Mt. Blanc glaciers and is used as an approach to the Brouillard ridge. Both sides of the pass are exposed to stonefall, sometimes bad. For Brouillard (E) side see Route 84. First traverse: G. B. and G. F. Gugliermina with N. Shiavi and Nicola Motta, 23-26 August, 1899.

85 W side.   AD.   From the Quintino Sella hut traverse E across the slopes of the little glacier which runs parallel with the rocks on which the hut stands. On the other side ascend a little over rocks and continue traversing in the same line across three rounded buttresses and three couloirs separating them (some avalanche risk) to reach the Mt. Blanc glacier (1½ h.). Cross the crevassed glacier, detours normally necessary, slightly downwards to the foot (pt. 3327) of the long couloir rising to Col Emile Rey. Climb this couloir, average angle 46° with steeper bits, by its snow/ice bed, or use rocks as convenient on the R side, to reach the col; stonefall (2-3½ h., 3½-5 h. from hut).

MONT BROUILLARD   4069m.   4068m. IGM

Below Col Emile Rey the Brouillard glacier is dominated by the lower continuation of the Brouillard ridge. From N to S the principal features of the ridge are Mont Brouillard, the highest pt., Pte. (Punta) Baretti (4013m., 4006m. IGM), Col du Brouillard (3288m.) and the Aigs. Rouges du Brouillard (3368m.), which are six minor summits. Mt. Brouillard itself can be easily reached from Col Emile Rey in 20 min. There are few worthwhile routes on the other peaks of the ridge. First ascent Mt. Brouillard: K. Blodig and O. Eckenstein with A. Brocherel, 11 July, 1906. P. Baretti: K. Blodig with L. Croux, 17 July, 1907.

COL ECCLES c. 4000m.

Between Pic Eccles (4041m.) and the lower part of the final section of the Innominata ridge. The col is of no particular interest as a passage, but is an important feature of several routes on this side of Mt. Blanc. First traverse: Eustace Thomas with J. Knubel and L. Proment, 9 July, 1928.

COL DE FRÊNEY c. 3600m.

Not marked on map. Between Pic Eccles and Pta. Innominata. A prominent snow shoulder above the col is pt. 3680m. A possible connection between the Frêney and Brouillard glaciers, but seldom used as such. See Route 17 for the ascent from the Brouillard glacier. The Frêney side is steep and loose. First traverse: G. Gruber with Emile Rey and P. Revel, 13-14 August, 1880.

PUNTA INNOMINATA 3729m.

The highest pt. (NW) of the lower section of the Innominata ridge, overlooking the Châtelet glacier. The SE summit (3620m.), from which the S and SE ridges descend, is visible from the Monzino hut. A longish easy ridge connects the SE and NW summits; the latter is just S of the Col de Frêney. The Innominata is a popular peak with pleasant training climbs; superb views of the Frêney and Brouillard faces of Mt. Blanc. First ascent: A. Durazzo with J. Grange and S. Henry, 23 July, 1872.

<u>South Ridge</u>. The longest and most interesting route. AD. First ascent: P. Preuss and U. di Vallepiana, 28 July, 1913.

86 From the Monzino hut climb the moraines (track) to reach the Châtelet glacier. Go up the glacier to the R and cross a short barrier of smooth wet rocks to reach the scree slope below the S face of the mtn. Climb scree and broken rocks, trending to the L, to reach the S ridge at the foot of its first big gendarme. Follow the ridge and avoid the gendarme by a horizontal traverse R (III). Avoid the next gendarme on the R, first by a ledge then by a chimney (III) which leads back to the ridge. Continue along the ridge over a third easier gendarme. From the gap after this traverse L for a few m. on to the W face, and climb this trending L for 20m. to a loose secondary ridge leading to near the SE summit. Cross the latter and follow the easy ridge on snow and rock to the NW summit ($4\frac{1}{2}$-$5\frac{1}{2}$ h. from hut).

<u>South-East Ridge</u>. The normal route, usually used for descent. PD. First ascent: E. Mackenzie with L. Croux and C. Ollier, 28 August, 1895.

87 From the Monzino hut follow Route 86 to the scree slopes below the S face of the mtn. Trend up to the R on mixed ground to reach the lower part of the SE ridge where it becomes well defined. Follow the crest easily on snowy rocks, turning a gendarme on either side, and finally keeping R of the crest up to the SE summit. Continue along the mixed ridge to the main summit (4-5 h. from hut).

From the Col de l'Innominata (Route 18) one can climb the whole of the SE ridge. From the col a short steep section (IV) is followed by a long easy traverse to join the route above.

COL DE L'INNOMINATA 3205m.

Between Pta. Innominata and Aig. Croux. A small col divided in two by a small gendarme. The most practical passage from the Monzino hut to the Frêney glacier above its most crevassed section. See Route 18. First traverse: H. O. Jones and G. W. Young with J. Knubel and J. Truffer, 12 August, 1912.

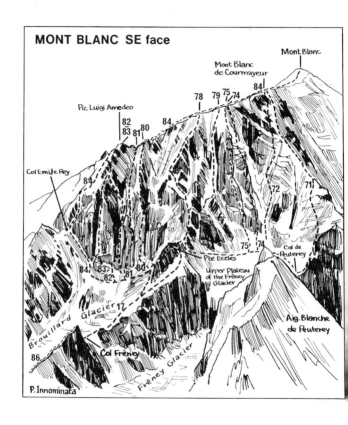

AIGUILLE CROUX 3256m.

An impressive rock buttress which terminates the lower part of the Innominata ridge. In addition to the routes described below there are at least two other very hard climbs on the E side. First ascent: Mlle. M. Mazzucchi with J. and H. Croux, 25 August, 1900.

<u>North-West Ridge.</u> A short connection from the Col de l'Innominata. AD. First ascent: M. Magni, E. Santi and M. Tedeschi, 10 September, 1907.

88 From the Col de l'Innominata (Route 18) climb directly up the first loose tower by a diagonal crack (10m., III). Continue along the ridge on better rock, traversing several small gendarmes. The last pitch on to the summit block is a curious overhang on the Frêney side ($1-1\frac{1}{2}$ h. from col).

<u>South Ridge.</u> The normal route and usually used for descent by abseils from pegs in place. AD with short pitches of IV on the crux slab. Note: the ridge can be climbed from its base direct, giving additional pitches of III up to the gap where it is joined by the usual route. First ascensionists.

89 From the Monzino hut climb the moraines and the Châtelet glacier to below the couloir leading to the Col de l'Innominata. Climb diagonally R on snow and broken slabs on to the SW face. Trend to the R and climb an ill defined shallow couloir (but several lines possible) to reach a small col in the S ridge. Above the col climb a smooth slab first by a thin crack (IV), then a bit of slab (III+) followed by another crack (IV) leading to an easier slab. Trend a little L near the top and reach a shoulder on the NW ridge a few min. from the summit. The slab is descended by two abseils (2-3 h. in ascent; $1\frac{1}{2}$-2 h. in descent).

<u>South-East Face.</u> An excellent training climb on mainly good

rock, technically quite difficult but the easiest line on this side of the buttress. The route follows the steep profile of the face seen from the Monzino hut and finishes on the S ridge at the foot of its key slab pitch. TD-, pitches of V graded with the use of pegs. Some moves technically A1. First ascent: E. Hurzeler and A. Ottoz, 5 July, 1935.

90 From the Monzino hut traverse across grass slopes and moraine to the E to reach a small snowfield at the foot of the SE face. Start from the extreme R of the snow and climb broken slabs (III) to reach a corner overlooking the Frêney glacier (1 h.).

Climb direct for a few min. until the rock steepens, then traverse up L to reach the foot of a black chimney which marks the line of the route. Avoid the first section by an awkward pitch on the L (25m.), then traverse almost horizontally above overhangs (V, 2 pegs) to rejoin the chimney. Climb the chimney for 50m. (IV and V) until it broadens into a forked couloir. Take the L branch to a bulging wall split by a chimney/crack. Climb this crack direct (V, A1, wet), or avoid it by an equally difficult pitch on the R, returning L along a ramp to climb another wall (V, pegs) before regaining the chimney. Continue up a deep chimney (IV) and a steep wall with an exit L (V). Follow an easier chimney to a steep slab of poor rock. Climb this trending R at first then L all the way (V) to enter an easy couloir leading to the small col in the S ridge. Continue as for Route 89 (5-6 h., 6-7 h. from hut).

COL DE PEUTEREY 3934m.

Between Mt. Blanc de Courmayeur and the Aig. Blanche de Peuterey. This magnificent col is described as an approach to the Frêney face climbs. See also Route 71 for the approach by the traverse of the Aig. Blanche. First traverse: J. Harlin and G. Hemming, 27-28 August, 1961.

<u>From the Frêney Glacier by the Rochers Gruber.</u> A complex route, exposed to stonefall on the Rochers Gruber. This is the quickest and best bad weather descent from the Col de Peuterey, but in poor visability route finding is difficult. AD+. First ascent: G. Gruber with Emile Rey and P. Revel, 13-14 August, 1880.

91 From the Monzino hut follow Route 18 over the Col de l'Innominata to reach the Frêney glacier. Climb the very crevassed glacier, route line variable according to conditions, to reach the foot of the prominent rock buttress which forms the R side of the steep icefall at the head of the lower Frêney glacier. This is the Rochers Gruber. Climb this buttress somewhat R of the crest; several traversing movements and stonefall. Reach steep snow and climb this diagonally L to a sharp snow rib which is followed to easy snow slopes adjoining the col further R (5-7 h. from Monzino hut).

In descent: From the col go SSW over gradually steepening snow and join a snow rib becoming quite steep and very narrow. Just short of the rock, descend L down steep snow until a rock step develops below. Now work R to reach a descent line marked by abseil pegs in place. Follow these trending somewhat R (facing out) all the way to the Frêney glacier at the bottom.

<u>From the Brenva Glacier by the North-East Couloir.</u> A serious climb because of stonefall danger, otherwise not of a high standard technically. D-, with pitches of IV. 550m. It is essential to reach the upper rock pitches before dawn. In recent times climbed frequently as the most practical approach to the Frêney pillars. First ascent: G. and M. Herzog with G. Rébuffat and L. Terray, 15 August, 1944. First winter ascent: R. Desmaison and R. Flematty, 1 February, 1967. Solo: P. Desailloud, 15-16 February, 1967.

AIG. BLANCHE DE PEUTEREY
N face

Brèche N des Dames Anglais

Pte. Gugliermina

L'Épée

Pointes SE

Pointe Central

Pointe NW

Col de Peuterey

71

93

93 note

93

92

92

Eckpfeiler

Brenva Glacier

92 From the Fourche or Trident huts the best approach is across Col Moore (Route 60). From the col go up the initial snow ridge of the Brenva spur for a short way, then turn off L and descend steep snow under the lowest rocks and over a bergschrund into the S bay of the upper Brenva glacier. From here a short nearly horizontal traverse on snow (avalanches from above) leads to the foot of the Eckpfeiler buttress flanked by the couloir (2 h.). Start up the couloir on its R side, then traverse into the centre. Climb two short steep walls then trend back R under the rocks of the Eckpfeiler. Climb keeping near these rocks to below the final rock wall barring the exit from the couloir. Up to this pt. several bergschrund features are crossed. Make a rising traverse L to the wall and climb this by a series of ascending ledges to reach a ridge on the L. Go up the ridge with two pitches of IV to slopes adjoining the col (4-5 h., 6-7 h. from huts).

AIGUILLE BLANCHE DE PEUTEREY 4112m.

A beautiful mtn. dominating the Frêney and Brenva glaciers. It has three summits linked by fine snow crests: NW (4104m. IGM), Central (4112m.), SE (4107m., 4108m. IGM). Conspicuous buttress lines on the wall overlooking the Frêney glacier have been climbed but are not recommended on account of poor rock and serious stonefall.
First ascent: H. Seymour King with Emile Rey, A. Supersaxo and A. Anthamatten, 31 July, 1885. First winter/spring ascent: H. Hoerlin and E. Schneider, 31 March, 1929.

Normal Route. This is represented by the first part of the Peuterey ridge route to Mt. Blanc. See Route 71.

North Face. A magnificent ice climb in splendid surroundings. The condition of the central sérac barrier determines the difficulty and objective danger of the original route, which turns the barrier on the L. The barrier can be turned on the

R by an independent line which has been followed less frequently and may be easier. D+, average angle 47° with sections up to 55°. 700m. First ascent: R. Chabod and A. Grivel, 4 September, 1933. (R-hand route: M. Bastien, M. Coutin, C. Gaudin and P. Julien, 6 July, 1952). Second ascent and first continued by Peuterey ridge to Mt. Blanc: Hermann Buhl and M. Schliessler, 10 August, 1949. First winter ascent: L. Belfrond and A. Ollier, 18 March, 1961. First British ascent: C. J. Phillips and E. Jones, 20 August, 1969 ($3\frac{1}{4}$ h. for face and descent from Col de Peuterey by Rochers Gruber). First solo (R-hand): D. Roulin, 19 August, 1973. Solo (L-hand): J. Afanassieff, 20 August, 1973 (Trident hut to top of Mt. Blanc in 9 h.).

93 L-hand Original Route. From the Trident/Fourche huts approach exactly as for Route 92, to the foot of the Peuterey couloir (2 h.). Traverse L on the glacier and climb the steep broken snow slope below the hanging glacier halfway up the face and in line between the two main summits. Trend L to reach a steep snow rib above a rocky part, which in turn runs into the wall of the hanging glacier at its L side. The wall has been generally climbed on the R by two or three steep ice pitches, but in favourable conditions it can be mainly outflanked to the L by relatively easy climbing. Above the barrier continue in a direct line on snow to a large bergschrund, troublesome after mid-season. Cross this and go up the steepening summit slope of snow/ice between several small bulges to the saddle linking the SE and Central summits (4-6 h., 6-8 h. from huts).

POINTE (PICCO) GUGLIERMINA 3893m.

A fine rock tower on the SE ridge of the Aig. Blanche. Immediately behind it is a slender needle, the Epée (3878m.

VT). See below. First ascent: G. B. Gugliermina and F. Ravelli, 23-24 August, 1914.

<u>South-West Face</u>. Frequently called the Gervasutti Pillar. An outstanding free climb on excellent rock, one of the best of its style in the Mt. Blanc range. TD+, 600m. Sustained climbing at V/V+ generally with few pegs in place. Only a fast party will avoid a bivouac and there are few good bivouac places on the route. First ascent: G. Boccalatte and G. Gervasutti, 17-18 August, 1938. First British (sixth) ascent: H. G. Nicol and E. A. Wrangham, 12 August, 1953. First solo: R. Shaw, 1971. First winter ascent: A. Anghileri, G. Lanfranconi, Maccarinelli and Valsecchi, over 4 days in January, 1975.

94 From the Monzino hut follow Routes 18, 71 over the Col de l'Innominata to the ledge line above the Frêney glacier running up to the diagonal Schneider couloir taken by Route 71. There are good bivouac sites on these ledges with running water. Stonefall possible (4 h. from hut). It is advisable to continue along the ledges and up the pitch giving access to the couloir so as to be able to recognise it in descent. A confident party can leave their bivouac gear on these ledges.

From a pt. about halfway along the ledge line go straight up on steep rocks at first, then on slabs. Trend generally to the R to reach by a final traverse R of 30m. the foot of an obvious steep pillar rising out of the slabs (150m., var. pitches of III, IV and one of IV+). Climb the crest of the pillar for 7 or 8 pitches (sustained, IV, V, V+) up to a detached flake. Climb the chimney either side formed by the flake (V+), exit R and continue up a dièdre trending R to a ledge (V). Above, the pillar merges into the very steep upper part of the face. The route avoids this by a rising traverse L across the head of a narrow gully L of the pillar (V).

Above the gully scrambling for a few min. leads to blocks

just below the pt. where the pillar merges into the upper face, which is marked by a conspicuous pointed rock up to the L. Directly below the latter climb a steep little wall by a groove (VI- or A1) to the pointed rock, awkward stance. From here make a difficult diagonal abseil L for 12m. across ribs and grooves to reach a small terrace (V/V+). Now follow a series of ledges rising L into short cracks which are taken (IV and V+ or A1) to broken rocks leading to the SW ridge which bounds the L-hand side of the face. On the L side of this ridge climb walls and slabs (IV with moves of V) trending R until easier rocks lead to the summit (7-9 h. from bivouac ledges).

Descent: Climb and abseil down the NW face to the gap between P. Gugliermina and the Epée, a conspicuous needle on this side of the mtn. Continue down broken slabs to join Route 71. Follow this down scree and broken rocks, then traverse R to reach the SE ridge near a conspicuous gendarme at the head of the Schneider couloir, then as for Route 71 down to the bivouac ledges (2-3 h.).

<u>South Face Direct</u>. Orientation SSE. A fine sustained route on good red granite. It follows a poorly marked pillar, R of the compact section of the S face. After taking a crack system higher up it continues directly to the summit and to the L of a large dièdre easily seen from below. ED-, pitches of V+ and VI, A1. 40 pegs and 2 wedges used on first ascent: D. Belden and A. Mroz, 11-13 July, 1971. Second ascent: L. and M. Bize, J. M. Cambon and G. Petriguet, 27-28 July, 1974.

95 Start as for Route 94, from which it would seem that it is best to bivouac on the ledges running up to the Schneider couloir. The first ascensionists made an original approach from the Frêney glacier below the ledge line, and entered and crossed the couloir at its lower end.

Continue to the end of the ledges and enter the couloir by a grade III pitch (Route 71). Almost immediately climb L up a

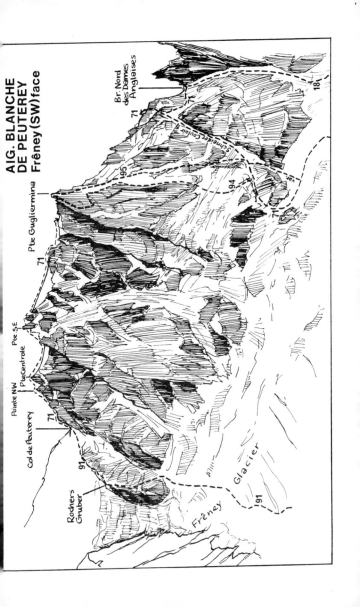

AIG. BLANCHE DE PEUTEREY Frêney (SW) face

Br. Nord des Dames Anglaises

18

71

71

S. Emile Couloir

195

94

Pte Gugliermina

71

Pte SE

Pte Centrale

Pointe NW

71

Col de Peuterey

71

91

Rochers Gruber

91

91

Frêney Glacier

vague spur to the R of overhanging rock to reach the big cracks in the lower part of the face. Climb these, aiming for a conspicuous flake situated slightly R of centre in the compact wall. Take a crack on the R and ascend it to a dièdre formed by the flake (IV+). Climb the dièdre (50m., IV, V) to a ledge at the top. From the R-hand end climb a shorter dièdre (IV+) to another ledge. (bivouac).

A chimney line above now marks the route. Climb it passing two overhangs (VI, V+) to belay under a third overhang. Move R for 2m. (V+) and climb a wall (IV+) to the R to reach another dièdre in 40m. (IV). Climb a wall formed by slabs for 20m. (V-). Below the second overhang exit L up a short overhanging dièdre (5m., A1, pegs). Continue more or less straight up for 40m. (IV, one traversing movement, V) to the first ledge system. Climb a deep crack in the wall to the L (30m., V, strenuous) to the second ledge system. Move up ledges for 40m. to the R to an enormous detached block on the crest of the vague pillar. From here a continuous system of cracks and dièdres cuts the upper part of the face.

Start up the first crack. After 10m. surmount an overhang (A1, pegs) and continue for 15m. (V, VI) to another overhang (V+, VI) which in turn is followed by 15m. (V, VI), leading to a large overhang. Start up this direct and finish on the R (A1, pegs). At the top go L to a good stance on a sloping slab. Continue up the dièdre for another pitch (V+), then bear L up a short wall (V) and finish up an easier wall (IV+) at a comfortable ledge. Trend R up the L side of the summit ridge for 40m. to the top (20-24 h. from bivouac below Schneider couloir).

BRÈCHE NORD DES DAMES ANGLAISES 3490m.

Between the Aig. Blanche and the Dames Anglaises. The approach from the Frêney glacier (Monzino hut) is described in Route 18, to reach the bivouac hut on the col. The Brenva side is a long steep snow couloir, very exposed to stonefall, and is of little use. First traverse: Mlle. S. Metzeltin, B. Crepaz and P. Pozzi, 25-26 July, 1960.

From the Brèche Sud des Dames Anglaises. Described as a link in the traverse of the complete Peuterey ridge. AD. First traverse: A. Goettner, F. Krobath and L. Schmaderer, 30 July, 1934.

96 From the Brèche S climb easy rocks on the crest line then keep on the Frêney side up to a shoulder at the foot of the vertical walls of Pte. Casati. Descend broken rocks on the Frêney side, then keep R down walls and grooves towards the couloir issuing from the Brèche N, which is reached below its junction with the branch from the Brèche Centrale. Climb the couloir to the Brèche N (3-4 h.).

LES DAMES ANGLAISES

Five elegant rock needles: the Isolée (3577m.), and the Ptes. Casati (3592m.), Crétier (3574m.), Castelnuovo (3601m., misprinted on IGN as 3610m.), and Yolande (3593m.). The Isolée is separated from the others by the Brèche Centrale (3503m.). The needles give short hard climbs.

BRÈCHE SUD DES DAMES ANGLAISES 3429m. 3435m. IGM

Between the Dames Anglaises and the Aig. Noire. The col has never been completely traversed. The ascent from the Frêney glacier is straightforward but exposed to stonefall.

AIGUILLE NOIRE DE PEUTEREY 3772m. 3773m. IGM

An enormous rock spire, one of the most beautiful in the Alps. It affords some of the most enjoyable and difficult climbs in the range. Nowadays the classic S ridge is climbed as frequently as the ordinary E ridge route. Few summits of this stature in the Alps have a route with the interest and quality of the Noire S ridge which becomes after only a few decades almost the normal way to the top.

First ascent: Lord Wentworth with Emile Rey and J.-B. Bich, 5 August, 1877. First winter ascent: H. Hoerlin, E. Schneider and H. Schroder, 16 March, 1929. First traverse: C. Negri, M. and C. Santi, 7 August, 1920.

<u>South Ridge</u>. One of the most interesting rock climbs of its standard in the Alps. It is sought after in the modern classic category represented by climbs such as the Badile Cassin route, Salbitschijen S ridge, Cima Grande Cassin route and La Meije S face direct. The ridge rises step-like in a series of picturesque towers with separate names. Many pitches are variable, even at the hardest sections, and route finding might be a problem although boot-marked rock and pegs invariably assist. The technical difficulties are not great and are separated by long stretches of easier pleasant climbing. The rock is generally excellent. However, the route is long, close to 1200m. and parties must move well together on the easier sections to avoid a bivouac on the ridge itself. A party that has passed the abseil from Pte. Welzenbach may find it difficult to retreat.

In pristine condition with half a dozen pegs, TD+. With three dozen pegs in key pitches, TD-. Most of the climbing is delicate with slab type moves. Regrettably the route is often overpegged, to the extent that parties have found up to 100 pegs in place, reducing the difficulty to D. The route is periodically depegged by the Courmayeur guides. Insecure pegs constitute a positive danger (several fatal accidents) and care must be exercised.

First ascent: K. Brendel and H. Schaller, 26-27 August, 1930. First winter ascent: Toni Gobbi and H. Rey, 26-27 February, 1949. First British ascent: G. C. Band, R. R. E. Chorley, G. H. Francis and E. A. Wrangham, 5-6 August, 1952. First solo: M. May, 1955.

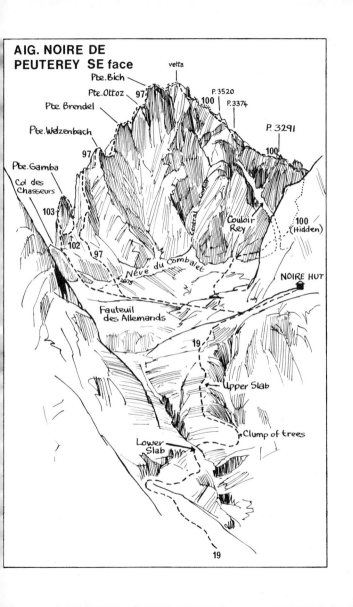

AIG. NOIRE DE
PEUTEREY SE face

vetta

Pte.Bich

97

Pte.Ottoz

100

P.3520

P.3374

Pte.Brendel

P.3291

Pte.Welzenbach

100

97

Pte.Gamba

Col des
Chasseurs

Central Couloir

Couloir
Rey

100
(Hidden)

103

102

97

Névé du Combalet
2075

NOIRE HUT

Fauteuil
des Allemands

19

Upper Slab

Clump of trees

Lower
Slab

19

97 From the Noire hut cross the Fauteuil des Allemands and go up a moraine to the foot of Pte. Gamba (3067m.), the lowest tower on the ridge (1 h.). Just L of pt. 2675 start climbing the rocks of the E spur of Pte. Gamba. After some 50m. climb a slab on the R (IV) then continue up grassy cracks and slabs, keeping slightly L to reach grassy ledges. All this section can be wet. Follow the ledges R to enter the couloir running down from the gap to the R of Pte. Gamba. Up to this pt. other ways are possible. Climb the couloir for about 30m., then mount the rib which divides it into two branches. Climb the rib for 50m. then cross the R-hand couloir. Now start up the wall of the next main tower, Pte. Welzenbach, by following a grassy ledge to its R-hand end, then climbing direct for 20m., then moving R to reach a rib descending from the two gendarmes which form the Second Tower under Pte. Welzenbach. Climb its crest at first then the L-hand side to reach a steep step near the top of the rib. Ledges. This marks the start of difficulties (2 h.).

Turn the step on the R and continue to climb two chimneys (IV) to near the top of the tower. Climb over several blocks and a slab (IV). Climb another block (IV) then after a bit of ridge an overhanging block, normally done with a shoulder (IV). Descend a slab on the R to reach a gap which separates the two gendarmes forming the Second Tower. Turn the second gendarme on its R side and rejoin the ridge crest. Keep R past another gendarme, and from a small gap beyond continue up a slab and small teeth (bits of IV) to a step which forces one to the R. Make an easy ascending traverse on ledges for 60m. to the R, then return L by slabs, one pitch of IV called the Welzenbach Slab, and a chimney to rejoin the ridge. Follow the crest to Pte. Welzenbach (3355m.) (3-4 h.).

Descend 20m. on the R side and abseil to the col between Pte. Welzenbach and Pte. Brendel. Traverse slightly R and go up for 25m. in a couloir. Return L-wards up a slabby ramp to rejoin the ridge and work on to the L side of the crest, along to the foot of a steep step - the Half-Moon Buttress. Stride over a gap and climb on good holds just L of the crest (V, several pegs) to belay below a small overhang. Move R on a ledge and take a groove to the large ledge on the flat top of the step (V). There are other ways up this section, technically slightly easier but seldom with many pegs in place, and the direct route described is normally slightly easier because of the extent of pegging. Continue up broken rocks on the ridge to the foot of a groove on the L. Climb the groove by steep slabs L (IV), and continue up a crack line in a smooth slab, avoiding an overhang by moving L (V) to reach ledged rocks. Continue more easily on broken rocks to the top of Pte. Brendel (3497m.) (2-3 h., good bivouac site).

Descend on the L side to the next gap, divided by a 10m. pillar of broken red rock. Traverse round its base on the L and climb a short chimney on the far side to its top (IV). Step on to the vertical wall of the Fifth Tower and climb trending L on small holds to reach the foot of a large smooth dièdre (V, small stance and peg belays). Climb the groove for about 35m. (V, pegs). At its top and below overhangs traverse R across an awkward sloping slab (V/V+, depending on the number of pegs and slings in place) to rejoin the ridge. Continue on easier rocks past bivouac sites, keeping to the R to reach the summit of the Fifth Tower, called by the Italians, Pte. Ottoz (3586m.). The summit can be by-passed by a traverse on the R to the gap behind the tower. Continue easily to the foot of a steep high step, defended at its base by a slab zone.

Start just R of the ridge line, climb a thin crack then two small overhangs (V, pegs). Continue trending R for 15m. then climb a chimney to arrive on the L of a large detached block. Climb straight up for 3m. to rejoin the ridge by a slabby ledge. Follow the ridge keeping L to a flat shoulder (good bivouac site). Climb cracks slanting up to the R at 45° to reach a couloir (IV). Or traverse R for 30m. to enter the couloir lower down, awkward. Climb the couloir to its top and continue up a short chimney to rejoin the ridge which is followed keeping L to the top of Pte. Bich (3753m.) (4-5 h.).

An abseil of 25m. and a short scramble lead to the gap before the summit of the Noire. Descend several m. on the R side, then climb scree ledges and broken rock to the R then back L to reach the summit (1 h., 12-16 h. from Noire hut. Best time for a roped party, 5½ h.).

West Face, Boccalatte Route. Joins the S ridge just above the Fifth Tower. A superb and sustained climb, more difficult at present though not as fine a line as the Direct Route. Unlikely to become popular because of a continuing vogue for the latter. TD/TD+ with pitches of V and one of VI. 500m. to S ridge. Excellent rock and mainly free climbing. Few pegs are in place - 24 used on first ascent: Nina Pietrasanta and G. Boccalatte, 1 August, 1935. Second ascent: L. Audoubert, M. Galy and G. Panozzo, 1 August, 1970.

98 From the Monzino hut follow Route 18 across the Col de l'Innominata, and traverse to the opposite side of the Frêney glacier under the couloir of the Brèche S des Dames Anglaises. Start at the foot of the face about 50m. R of the bergschrund of this couloir (3-4 h.).

Climb trending R for 10m. to a ledge. Towards the R take a groove for 20m. (IV+) to a large earthy gangway. From the R-hand end climb a crack with jammed blocks at 6m. (IV) and 20m. (V, peg) to a platform on the R. Now stride L into an overhanging crack (IV+) and climb this, then a wall and a short chimney (IV) on the R. Continue direct for 30m. (IV) to easier ground on the L. Go up this L then R to reach a level saddle in a spur formed on the R. (This is where the Direct Route diverges). On the R side of the spur is a large scree couloir.

Descend into this and ascend it for 50m. until it narrows almost to a crack flanked by smooth walls. The couloir is the lower continuation of the huge overhanging groove descending from the gap L of Pte. Bich. Some 50m. to the R and above is another crack system running up the side of a smooth vertical spur. This is the line of the route.

From the couloir narrows make a rising traverse R over smooth slabs (IV) and cross a couloir. Continue in the same line on easier loose rock, then traverse R across a pleasant wall (IV) to a ledge at the foot of the crack system, normally wet. Climb the wide crack for 15m. to an overhang which is taken direct (V/V+). About 8m. higher climb another overhang (V/VI, pegs), above which is a large detached block. Continue up a delicate groove for 20m. (VI then IV+). A slightly easier groove leads to a short chimney in turn closed by a large wet overhang. Traverse L below this on a slab (IV+) into a vertical groove and climb this for a few m. to make a long stride R to rejoin the crack (V+). Ledge higher up. Above climb a small overhang followed by an easier couloir running up to a band of sloping ledges. Follow the ledges and slabs trending R towards the S ridge. This movement becomes progressively a traverse of the wall. Keep moving R over several delicate sections. A long slab is followed by a steep wall (V-), then more slabs R lead to a small couloir. Go up this to the S ridge at the foot of the step above the Fifth Tower (10 h.). Follow Route 97 to the summit ($2\frac{1}{2}$ h., about 16 h. from Monzino hut).

West Face, Direct Route. A magnificent climb on generally good rock. The main difficulties are concentrated in the upper section of the climb. The original route included a hard artificial pitch which can be avoided. More than sufficient pegs will usually be found in place. Only a fast party will avoid a bivouac on the descent. TD with pitches of V/V+ and

A1. 650m. First ascent: V. Ratti and L. G. Vitali, 18-20 August, 1939. First British (fifth) ascent: T. D. Bourdillon and H. G. Nicol, 1955. First winter ascent: A. Bozzetti and L. Pramotton, 31 January - 2 February, 1967. First solo ascent: G. Bertone, 2 July, 1975 in 6 h.

99 Start as for Route 98 and reach the rock saddle in a spur on the lower part of the face. Move up the spur for a few m. then traverse L to below a series of cracked slabs. Climb these to the top of the buttressed spur with pleasant pitches of III/IV. Continue along a fine snow crest to rocks leading to the main wall of the face. Beyond a gap climb one pitch then traverse L across a small couloir, followed by an ascending traverse L to a larger couloir. Climb this couloir by a series of chimneys and grooves, first with an overhang (IV+) then below an overhanging L wall beside a groove (IV+). Exit L over slabs to a platform below the crux section.

From a flake on the R climb the bed of an initial groove, then on the L, and over a bulge in the middle to a chockstone (hard) which leads to a short strenuous chimney giving access to a good stance above and to the L (30m., V/V+, pegs). The next cracked groove is the first part of the Dièdre of Suffering. Start up a crack R of the bed (V, A1) and join the crack in the back of the groove (A1) which overhangs higher up. After 20m. from the stance exit diagonally R below the main overhang by a crack between it and the R wall. Traverse 5m. R to another crack. Climb this for 8m. (IV+). Above this are the continuation cracks of the main dièdre (VI), which are normally avoided as follows. Traverse R across a very exposed wall for 15m. (V, pegs) to a crack. Take this up a short wall (V, pegs) to a stance. Continue up the steep wall by cracks and flakes for a few m. then trend L to a series of terraces above the main groove.

Cross the terraces in a short rising traverse L to a couloir. Take this for two pitches (IV) and exit L at an overhang (IV+).

Then a short crest leads R to a corner giving access (IV) to a gap a few m. R of the summit (8-12 h. from bergschrund, 12-16 h. from Monzino hut).

West Face, other routes

Dièdre Route to main summit tower.
G. Bertone and R. Desmaison, 3-5 July, 1973. This is probably the least attractive route on the W face. It uses two enormous chimneys which cut first the R side then the L side of the depression running down from the saddle between the summit (L) and Pte. Bich (R). Near the top the route moves from the first chimney L across a very difficult wall under a line of big overhangs, and above a lower line of overhangs, to join the second chimney. This chimney was found to contain several recent pegs and karabiners in place. Rock generally very bad and the climbing dangerous. 650m. ED+, 150 pegs of all types and sizes used.

Direct Route to Pte. Bich.
J. Couzy and R. Desmaison, 3-4 August, 1957.
This is a major variation, albeit for the most part independent, of the Boccalatte Route 98. It takes a line of cracks and chimneys L of those used by the Boccalatte route in the middle section, and after these, instead of following a rising traverse R to the S ridge, continues more or less straight up to reach another series of grooves and cracks leading to a shoulder on the S ridge not far below Pte. Bich. Rock fairly good. 600m. ED with pitches of V, several bits of VI, and A1/2.

W Face of Pte. Brendel.

M. Claret and R. Desmaison, 13-15 August, 1973.

A pleasant slab route, reached from the sérac-torn Frêney glacier up a dièdre below the L side of a small hanging snowfield/depression in the face some 100m. above the glacier. From the snowfield the line trends L to the middle of a long slabby zone running up R then L and finally direct to the top. Good rock. 600m. ED-, pitches of V+ and A1/2.

W Face of Pte. Welzenbach.

G. Bertone, M. Claret and R. Desmaison, September, 1973. Communal start with previous route. From the head of snowfield route takes a direct line marginally to R of summit line to join the S ridge about three pitches below top of Pte. Welzenbach. Good rock. 500m. ED-, pitches of V and V+, and A1/2.

South-East Face of Pte. Bich

A direct route up this face was made by an Italian party in 1937, over 3 days, when several grade VI pitches were identified. The second ascent was made by A. Rouse and R. Carrington in 1975 in one day.

<u>East Ridge.</u>   The normal ascent and descent route, long and complicated.   Various ways up to and along the ridge are possible, and good route finding is essential to avoid losing time. The first ascensionists of the mtn. went up the large R to L diagonal couloir cutting the flank of the lower part of the ridge, and reached the latter just above the step, pt. 3374m. IGM, thereafter taking a series of traverses on the S side of the ridge to the top. This route by the Rey couloir is subject to stonefall and was used about 14 times up to 1902 and thereafter has been seldom done. It remains the shortest way. PD with pitches of II/II+.

In the whole of the upper part at least one distinctly separate line is practised for descent, which makes four semi-circular movements on the Fauteuil (S) side without touching the ridge crest until the latter is joined at the base (c. 3300m.) of the step, pt. 3374m. This has pitches of III normally abseiled in descent (not described).

The modern ascent route was first followed by E. Allegra with L. Mussillon and H. Brocherel, 27 July, 1902. It takes a line to the ridge well to the R of the Rey couloir. This first part has been the subject of fewer variations, but after that, along the ridge many variations have been done. It is longer and more complicated than the Hörnli ridge of the Matterhorn. The best course is to stay as close as possible to the ridge, more so in descent where abseil pegs and slings indicating short cuts off the ridge abound. Therefore while variable, the recommended descent route largely corresponds with the ascent.   PD with pitches of II/II+ and one of III if the correct way is found. Variations along the ridge or on the S side of it involve more pitches of III.

AIG. NOIRE DE PEUTEREY W face

vetta
Pointe Bich
97
99
97
101
99
P. Ottoz
P. Brendel
98
97
P. Welzenbach
98
18

100 From the Noire hut follow a track W and cross the inner stream, then go up moraine NW by a small track to the snow-field at the top and R of the broad rock spur coming down from the vicinity of pt. 3374 on the ridge high above. Climb towards an avalanche cone at the base of a secondary couloir situated midway between the great central couloir (L) and the Rey couloir (R). Just R of this secondary couloir climb grassy rocks trending L for 15m. to a track running R. Follow this over ledges and grassy slopes in a long traversing movement and in due course cross the base of the Rey couloir. Continue traversing R to the next couloir and cross this to the spur/ridge enclosing its R side. (This couloir rises to enter the Rey couloir higher up). Now climb a grassy slope on the R side of this ridge for about 100m., then move L to a small grass/scree saddle in the ridge. Work L into the secondary couloir and climb it for 40m. (stonefall possible) until loose earthy ledges on the R can be followed to rejoin the ridge at a notch above its narrowest section. Continue up the ridge with one pitch of III, becoming a spur of grassy broken rock, for 100m. to within 25m. of the main E ridge, at the base of a large square-shaped gendarme.

Climb diagonally L some 30m. below the ridge, over scree shelves and up a series of short couloirs, maintaining the rising traverse, and pass below a small hoof-shaped gendarme. Just after this climb directly towards the ridge and reach it about 50m. distance from a double gendarme (3291m. VT). Follow the ridge to the foot of the first tower, turn this on the R and reach the gap between the two. The second is turned on the L side by an ascending traverse for 50m. before rejoining the crest. Continue on the ridge, using ledges on the L side and climbing a chimney on this side, to the foot of a big step, the top of which is pt. 3374m. Descend a few m. L and traverse horizontally to a couloir. Climb its steep slabby bed (II+) for 80m. to scree bands under the ridge. Traverse up L on scree and broken rocks to reach the crest again below another big step (3520m. IGM). Turn this on the L along scree ledges then climb a chimney (II+) to a notch in the ridge about 30m. distance beyond the top of the step. Abseil pegs and old slings hereabouts. Follow the ridge, avoiding two small gendarmes by keeping generally on the R side over snow and slabs, up to a small shoulder at the foot of a vertical step. Traverse 70m. L over large loose blocks in a hollow, then climb a short couloir in a rockband. Continue direct up ledged rocks to a vague shoulder adjoining the crest. Keeping L of the crest go up cracks/chimneys in a staircase formation to join the crest above its last steep section and about 100m. of easy ground from the summit (6-7 h. from Noire hut. 4-5$\frac{1}{2}$ h. in descent).

North-North-West Ridge. A precipitous and very severe ridge in two big steps amid remote surroundings. The audacious and unrepeated ascent was made by J. Couzy and R. Desmaison, 23-25 July, 1956. ED and A3. It does not seem to be a route with anything to commend it. A variable descent route on the ridge is equally vicious and sensational, and takes a separate line from the climbing route. This descent is practised by parties engaged on the Peuterey integral ridge (see Routes 71, 96) and is made almost entirely by long, tricky and dangerous abseils which equate to at least D+. Serious stonefall danger on the lower step. An abseil rope of at least 80m. is necessary. First descent: A. Goettner, F. Krobath and L. Schmaderer, 29-30 July, 1934. First British descent: C. M. Gravina and S. G. McH. Clark, 27 July, 1956 (continued next day to Aig. Blanche and turned back by a storm). First winter descent: B. Allemand, J. Calcagno, A. Gogna and G. Macchetto, February, 1971. Descended solo by J. Coqueugniot and R. Desmaison in 1972.

101 Descent: From the summit abseil down very steep slabs and in a shallow couloir after some distance to the edge of the sheer drop overlooking the intermediate snow shoulder. Continue abseiling on one side of the crest line or the other, only a few m. from it, freely in space at the top, for 80m. to the shoulder. Very poor stances/changeover places. The best line seems to be the L side down to a snowy ledge in 30m. from the overhanging prow, and on the edge of the W face. After that easier abseiling in 50m. to the shoulder. Descend the shoulder for a short distance only keeping L, then commence abseiling down the lower step on its L (W) side in a huge chimney/couloir of 180m. This overhangs in several places and is very exposed to stonefall. At the bottom make a descending traverse R (facing out) down ledged rocks, then abseil down walls into the snow couloir of the Brèche S des Dames Anglaises. Climb this couloir by a rock rib in its centre to the col (5-6 h.).

PIC (POINTE) GAMBA 3067m.

A fine rock spire at the foot of the Noire S ridge, which constitutes the First Tower of that ridge. Short but worthwhile training climbs. First ascent: P. Preuss and U. di Vallepiana, 20 July, 1913.

<u>South Ridge and East Face</u>. The easiest route of ascent and descent. Interesting climbing on good rock. AD, pitches of III. 300m. First ascensionists.

102 From the Noire hut traverse the screes of the Fauteuil des Allemands and climb scree and snow slopes then a steep couloir to the N gap of the Col des Chasseurs (c. 2750m.) at the foot of the S ridge (1 h.).

From the col climb broken rocks and grass L for 40m. to the foot of a steep wall. Turn this by a short traverse L then climb back trending R to the ridge above the wall. Climb a 10m. chimney then broken rocks on the L side. Traverse horizontally for 25m. on the L (W) side then climb cracks to rejoin the ridge at a small shoulder. The excursion on to the E face commences here. Descend 50m. on the R side and traverse grass ledges to reach a small buttress which descends E from the summit. (This pt. can also be reached by a short connection from Route 97). Climb this buttress for 40m., traverse L, then continue more or less straight up on steep grassy rocks towards a small gap in the upper part of the S ridge. Pass a little R of this gap, then about 50m. below the summit go diagonally R and climb a slab by a crack. Traverse a ledge R and climb a chimney filled with loose blocks to the summit (3-4 h., 5-6 h. from hut).

<u>South Ridge Direct.</u> A fine climb on good rock. D with pitches of V. 300m. First ascent: A. Frattola and Toni Gobbi, 2 July, 1944.

103 From the Noire hut follow Route 102 to the foot of the steep wall in the lower part of the S ridge. Climb the wall by a diagonal crack (V) and follow the ridge to a small shoulder, where Route 102 descends on the R side. Climb the steepening ridge to a smooth nose. Take this for 3m. then traverse L (IV) and abseil 8m. into a small couloir. Climb this (IV) then climb fine walls, trending R then L to rejoin the ridge (IV). Continue more or less directly up the ridge to a bulge in the shape of a head (obvious from the Noire hut about two-thirds up the ridge). Climb this direct by a small couloir then short walls on the R (IV). Tiny stance further R. Continue up the ridge keeping slightly L up short walls and slabs (sustained, IV) to below a final barrier of yellow overhanging rocks. Just L of the ridge line climb a difficult and strenuous groove with an overhang (V), followed by broken rocks to the summit ($3\frac{1}{2}$-$5\frac{1}{2}$ h. from Col des Chasseurs).

154

COL DES CHASSEURS   2740m.

Between Pte. Gamba and Mont Rouge de Peuterey. The col is double with pt. 2802 dividing it. The col provides a link between the Monzino and Noire huts, but the approach on the Monzino side is on very steep and unpleasantly loose scree and rock slopes and the crossing of the Frêney glacier is at one of its most crevassed sections. See also Route 102. First traverse: Miss Overton, E. H. F. Bradby, J. H. Wicks and C. Wilson with Henri Rey, 19 July, 1905.

MONT ROUGE DE PEUTEREY   2941m.

The final rock bastion of the S ridge of the Aig. Noire. First ascent: E. H. F. Bradby, J. H. Wicks and C. Wilson, 26 July, 1905.

MONT NOIR DE PEUTEREY   2923m.   2928m. IGM

The final rock bastion of the E ridge of the Aig. Noire. First ascent: T. S. Kennedy and J. A. G. Marshall with U. Almer and J. Fischer, 17 July, 1873.

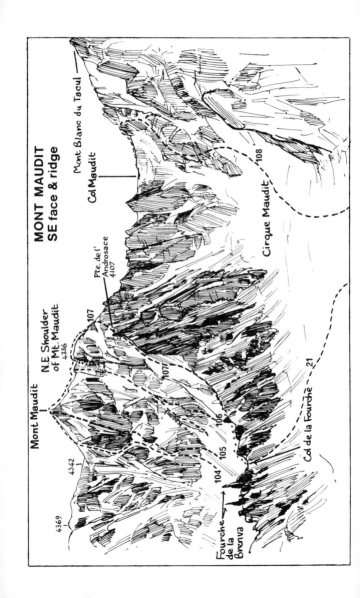

MONT MAUDIT
SE face & ridge

Mont Blanc du Tacul

Col Maudit

Cirque Maudit

108

Pte. de l'
Androsace
4107

N.E Shoulder
of Mt. Maudit
4336

107

Mont Maudit

107

4342

4369

106

105

104

Col de la Fourche

21

Fourche de la Brenva

Maudit · Tacul group

COL DE LA BRENVA   4303m.

Between Mt. Blanc and Mt. Maudit. The Brenva side is very steep and exposed to falling séracs. The French side is easy but complex. Not in fact used as a pass but as an exit pt. or landmark for other routes. See Routes 55,56. First traverse: G. S. Mathews, A. W. Moore, F. and H. Walker with J. and M. Anderegg, 15 July, 1865.

MONT MAUDIT   4465m.

A fine summit but rarely climbed for its own sake. The French side is a complex glacier slope broken by rock buttresses. The Italian face is an impressive 600m. wall of rock and ice with several fine routes. See Route 56 for the traverse of the main ridge (normal routes). First ascent: W. E. Davidson and H. Seymour Hoare with J. Jaun and J. von Bergen, 12 September, 1878.

South-East Face (Original Italian Route). This route takes the buttress L of the summit line and R of a large couloir depression rising to pt. 4342. The lower part of the buttress is split and the R-hand section is taken to more than halfway up the face. From its base this section is marked by a red pillar about 275m. high, and R of it is a triangular icefield directly below the summit. A serious climb with fairly continuous difficulties on rock and ice. D+/TD- with rock pitches of IV. 650m. It is reckoned harder than any of the Brenva face routes. First ascent: L. Binel, R. Chabod and A. Cretier, 4 August, 1929. First British ascent: J. L. Jones and A. Morgan, 1973. First winter ascent: J. P. Balmat & D. Ducroz; M. Dandelot & J. Jenny, 22-24 December, 1975.

104 From the Fourche/Trident huts descend as for Route 60 to the upper plateau of the Brenva glacier and go up to the

bergschrund system under the face (1-1¼ h.). Cross this
slanting R to L (in late season, very difficult) and climb a
short, very steep ice slope to the rocks. At the foot of the
pillar start up the first chimney in its L side, immediately R
of the couloir dividing the main buttress (L) and pillar (R).
(There is a large chimney line further R, being the start of
Route 105). Take this chimney for a few m. then climb L into
a groove which is followed for 30m. (IV) to a terrace. Just
R, follow another chimney (IV) to the crest of the pillar.
Climb this up slabs and short steep walls on good holds (III
and IV). After a smooth 10m. chimney (IV) the angle eases.
Avoid the last pillar step by easy rocks on the R and return L
to a fine snow crest behind the pillar. Climb the crest then
rocks behind it and L of a corner to a large gangway line
slanting L. Follow this over ice and snowy rocks to the crest
of the main buttress further L, which is reached just below an
overhanging snow pulpit. Turn the latter on the L and continue
up the ridge, rocky and very steep followed by a fine snow
crest with cornices on both sides. Go through an exit cornice
on to the main frontier ridge and continue easily to the summit
(6-10 h. from bergschrund).

South-East Face, Direct Route. A fine mixed route with the
rock climbing entirely free on excellent granite. Some stonefall danger. TD with pitches of V+. 750m. First ascent:
J. P. Bougerol and A. Mroz, 17-19 August, 1971. The route
was repeated with several harder variations (V+, A1) in 1975.

105 Start as for Route 104. About 20m. R of the entry chimney
for Route 104 is a dièdre. Climb this for 40m. (V, V+), then
a continuation dièdre for three pitches (IV, V+) to exit L to a
concealed gap in the pillar on this side. Climb the pillar,
Route 104 (IV), to a smooth wall. Move R (IV+) to a dièdre
just on the R side and go up this (15m., V-) to a broken zone
on the L. Climb this for 40m. then trend R and make a

slanting traverse R on mixed ground to reach a ridge on the L. Follow this for three pitches to an obvious gendarme which is turned on the R by a dièdre (III) to reach a couloir. Two pitches up the couloir (falling stones and ice) reach a zone of large slabs forming the central step of the face.

Move up L then R to a chimney groove not evident from below. Follow this with fine climbing up the middle of the slabs for two long pitches (IV, V+), then exit R below a depression which cuts the upper part of the step. Follow the L edge of the depression (one bit of V+) for 80m. About 10m. below a snowfield above, traverse R for 15m. then finish straight up.

Climb the snowfield towards the summit triangle for five mixed pitches, passing R of an enormous block. Start up the middle of the triangle by a broken groove (IV). Follow a groove system and ribs trending L to the main ridge about 25m. L of the summit (15 h. from bergschrund).

<u>South-East Face (Polish Route)</u>. The R-hand side of the face is bordered by a long buttress descending from L of pt. 4336 to a pt. in the glacier below and R of the start for Routes 104, 105. The lower part of this buttress is relatively massive and has been climbed in three ways to an easier middle section where all routes more or less join. The original route (Kagami, 1929) took the L side of the buttress (bad stonefall possible). The most direct way up it is near the crest, the route described below, and a major variation has been made between the two (Guilliard/Irvin, 1969). The topmost section should not be underestimated. A recent party reported they took 3 h. for the last 200m., albeit in bad conditions. The Polish route has only been climbed twice. The second ascensionists commented it must be the only line on this side of the face sheltered from stonefall. A serious mixed climb of 650m.

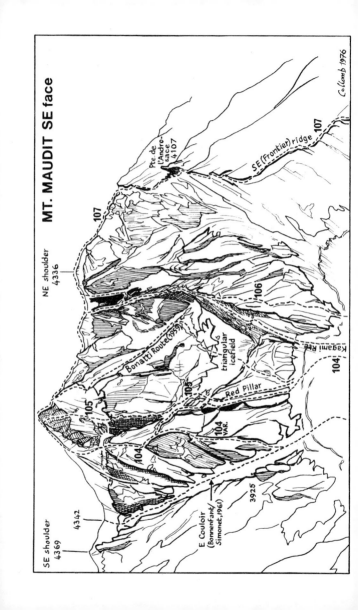

MT. MAUDIT SE face

SE shoulder 4369
4342
SE (Frontier) ridge
NE shoulder 4336
Pte. de L'Andro-sace 4107
107
107
107
106
Bonatti Route (1959)
triangular icefield
Kagami Rte.
104
105
105
Red Pillar
105
104 VAR.
104
104
3925
E Couloir (Bonnenfant/Simonet, 1961)
Collomb 1976

TD with pitches of V+/VI. 50 rock and 10 ice pegs used on first ascent: L. Sadus and R. Zawadski, 5-6 August, 1963.

106 Approach as for Route 104, cross the bergschrund and climb a short snow/ice slope to the lowest rocks of the buttress. Climb easy snowy rocks trending R to the foot of a chimney. Climb this, overhanging at the top, to a ledge. From the R-hand end of the ledge climb a crack slanting R to reach the top of a triangular block (V+). Continue by an easier crack then trend L and take a chimney/groove (V+/VI). Trend L again for another pitch, then back R slightly to the foot of an overhanging groove. Higher up this groove becomes a narrow chimney, obvious from the foot of the buttress, and which is well defined by steep walls on the L. Climb the groove (V+) then its L flank to reach the chimney. Take the chimney and walls to its L to reach a good ledge. Now climb diagonally R for 15m. and go up another shorter chimney filled with loose blocks. This is followed somewhat L by a further chimney in two pitches (V+, overhanging in parts) to the top of the buttress proper (7 h. from bergschrund).

Continue up the crest of the spur on snow and rock with numerous short obstacles to the foot of the final steep step in the ridge. Climb the step on its R side, not far from the couloir bordering the ridge on this side. Reach by steep climbing a snowhead (cornice) on the main NE ridge, which is followed to the summit in 1 h. (8 h., 15 h. on average from bergschrund). Note: The original Kagami route descended by abseil into the couloir beside the final step, which is very steep and can be very difficult in imperfect conditions, to finish by crossing this couloir and climbing a big chimney on its R side to exit on the summit ridge R of the snowhead.

South-East (Frontier) Ridge. Often called the Tour Ronde ridge of Mt. Maudit. One of the finest ridge routes of its class in the range. A long climb at high altitude with mainly

161

snow/ice difficulties.   D.   The upper part of the ridge is marked by a large rock tower, Pte. de l'Androsace (4107m.), the main obstacle on the climb.   This tower has a notable independent route on its E spur which rises out of the Cirque Maudit.   First ascent: M. von Kuffner with A. Burgener, J. Furrer and a porter, 2-4 July, 1887.   First British (third) ascent: R. L. G. Irving, G. L. Mallory and H. E. G. Tyndale, 18 August, 1911.   First winter ascent: L. and L. Pozzi with A. Ottoz, 28 March, 1949 (a better date in mid-February was only achieved in 1975).   First solo: J. H. Colle, 5 August, 1972.

107 From the Fourche biv. hut follow the ridge, at first horizontal and snow, then mixed with rocks, turning obstacles easily up to a thin snow crest running to the foot of the first step. Climb this by an ice couloir just R of the ridge, returning to the crest where it becomes snowy again. A similar couloir L of the ridge may be easier in dry conditions. Climb snow then a thin snow crest to a shoulder forming the top of the step. This crest continues for some distance up to the base of a large red gendarme, the Pte. de l'Androsace. In good or reasonable conditions (on some occasions found to be a "walk") turn the base of the gendarme by a traverse L on steep snow/ice mixed with rocks. Continue the traverse past the main gendarme and its next subsidiary pinnacles to rejoin the ridge at a small snow saddle after the last obstruction.

When conditions are bad for this traverse one must climb the Pte. de l'Androsace. Start up a deep chimney on the R, then a wall giving access to a short couloir emerging into slabby walls and cracks. Continue up these steeply to the top (several short bits of IV). Abseil off the top down the L (Brenva) side and continue over several pinnacles to the snowy saddle (adds 1 h. to normal route time).

Above is the second big step in the ridge. Climb steep mixed ground trending L for 25m. to enter a slanting couloir.

Go straight up this at first, then somewhat R and finally L to finish on the NE ridge of Mt. Maudit about 100m. below its shoulder pt. 4336m. Follow the ridge at first on the L side then slightly on the R, turning the summit rocks which are climbed from the W(R) side (5-8 h. from Fourche biv. hut).

COL MAUDIT 4035m.

Between Mt. Maudit and Mt. Blanc du Tacul. First traverse: T. Graham Brown with A. Graven and J. Knubel, 1 August, 1932.

<u>Descent to the Cirque Maudit glacier bay</u>. This may provide a useful descent, following the rocky spur on the true L bank of the couloir. Descended by first traverse party. AD.

108 From the foot of the SW ridge of Mt. Blanc du Tacul traverse across the top of the rocky spur forming the true L bank of the couloir further R. Descend the spur, keeping to its R (W) flank with one difficult chimney/couloir section, until above its final steepening. Traverse L (E) and cross the bergschrund at the foot of the S couloir depression of Mt. Blanc du Tacul ($2\frac{1}{2}$-3 h.). This leads into the glacier bay from where all hut routes over the Géant glacier are easily reached.

MONT BLANC DU TACUL 4248m.

A fine mtn. rendered totally accessible since the late 1950s following the construction of the cableway system across the range. It has two principal summits, the W and higher pt., and an E pt. which consists of two rocky pts. (4247m. and 4241m.).

The ordinary route is the NW side above the Col du Midi (described in descent, Route 56). This normally takes 3 h. in ascent. This is also the normal descent route after climbing the mtn. by other ways. Parties are warned that notwithstanding the features and normal conditions described in Route 56, this descent can become quite hazardous, especially in winter.

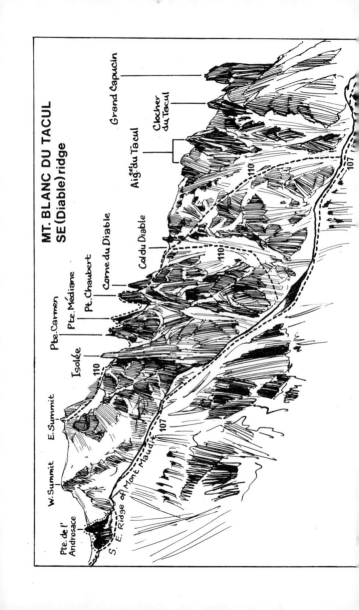

MT. BLANC DU TACUL
SE (Diable) ridge

Grand Capucin

Clocher du Tacul

Aig. du Tacul

Col du Diable

Corne du Diable

Pt. Chaubert

Pte. Médiane

Pte. Carmen

Isolée

E. Summit

W. Summit

Pte. de l' Androsace

S. E. Ridge of Mont Maudit

110

107

The snow slopes are steep and prone to avalanche and several long wide crevasses may have to be negotiated. Near the bottom the upper edge of the main bergschrund can rise 10m. above the lower, making an awkward abseil necessary. In good conditions, which may be hard to determine from above, one of the relatively short routes on the N facet of the mtn. may be better for descent - but in many cases parties have reported considerable difficulties on this facet - usually in the winter season.

The magnificent NE face of the mtn. has one of the finest close-knit collections of rock, ice and mixed routes in the range. These routes are increasing in popularity every year. The satellite summits standing out from the ridges enclosing the NE face are described separately.

First ascent: One or more members of the Hudson-Kennedy party, 8 August, 1855. First winter ascent not recorded.

109 North-West Face from Grands Mulets. This fine glacier route was described in the previous guide. Unfortunately the lower icefall entry between rock buttresses 3130m. (L) and 3099m. (R) has become exceedingly contorted and is hardly practicable. The middle and upper sections are still in reasonable condition. Formerly, AD. First ascent: A. Migot and J. Savard, 3 July, 1928.

South-East (Diable) Ridge Traverse. The SE ridge, after a straightforward drop of 150m., narrows to a jagged rock crest with five sharp pinnacle summits - the Aigs. du Diable. The traverse of these pinnacles gives a magnificent and popular expedition. A serious undertaking with some difficult and delicate climbing mostly over 4000m. Generally D-, but with numerous rock pitches of IV/IV+ and one avoidable one of V. Ways up to the ridge have been varied and only the normal approach is described below. First traverse: Miss M. E. O'Brien and R. L. M. Underhill with Armand Charlet and Georges Cachet, 4 August, 1928. First in winter (omitting Corne du Diable and the Isolée): Erika Stagni and M. Galley with Raymond Lambert, 9-10 February, 1938 (party rescued gravely frostbitten after first notable search operation arising from a serious winter mountaineering expedition).   First British traverse: G. G. Macphee with J. Burnet, 13 August, 1949 (without guides, Mr. & Mrs C. Smith, 1950). First solo: R. Chere, 27 July, 1974.

110 From the Torino hut follow Route 23 into the Cirque Maudit. Go up to the R, to the foot of a couloir in the SW side of the Diable ridge.   This is the second couloir to the L, counting from the Clocher tower (3853m.) at the lower end of the ridge. The couloir is distinctly R of one dropping straight down from the Col du Diable, at the foot of the first big tower (Corne du Diable) on the ridge.   Cross the bergschrund at c. 3580m. ($1\frac{1}{2}$ h.), climb the couloir for 125m. then trend L over snowy rocks and subsidiary couloirs to reach the Col du Diable (3955m.) by steep mixed terrain ($1\frac{1}{2}$ h.). Alternatively, the bergschrund can be crossed higher up, below a narrow buttress descending from the Corne du Diable. Ascend below it diagonally R and climb the steep snow/ice couloir directly below the Col du Diable.

Follow a thin snow ridge then traverse L-wards on easy ledges round the first needle (Corne du Diable), and climb to a small snow saddle adjoining Brèche Chaubert (4047m. VT) between it and Pte. Chaubert (30 min.). From this gap one can climb fairly easily (III) to the top of the Corne du Diable, returning to the gap by a short abseil (30 min.).

From the Chaubert gap climb a smooth slab (IV+) and easier rocks in the ridge line to the top of Pte. Chaubert (4074m.). Descend the NW face of this pinnacle by three abseils to the first gap of Brèche Mediane. Turn a gendarme on the R to enter the second and lower gap (4017m. VT), at the foot of Pte. Mediane (1 h.).

Trend slightly R up ledges then back L to the foot of a large open groove about 45m. high.   Climb the back of the groove for 10m. (IV), then make a short traverse horizontally R to a notch in the R bounding ridge. Climb a crack L of the ridge

166

for 15m. (IV) to a narrow platform. Traverse R for a few m. on the NE face then climb steep slabs direct for 10m. (IV) to rejoin the ridge. On the other side step down and cross the top of the groove. (Alternatively, the groove can be climbed direct, IV+, 3 pegs). The top of Pte. Mediane (4097m. VT) is composed of three large blocks resting against one another, forming two windows. Traverse the L side by three successive terraces and go through the far window. The top can be reached easily from this side ($1\frac{1}{2}$ h.).

Return to the third (last) terrace and go through the window tunnel on the R to emerge on the NW side. Abseil 25m. down this side then traverse across to Brèche Carmen (4057m. VT). Alternatively make a 30m. abseil from the L-hand window straight into the gap. Beware of the rope jamming. Now climb cracks (IV) on the R of the E ridge of Pte. Carmen and make a rising traverse R under its E top to the platform between its summits. Climb up and down the sharp ridge to the W top of Pte. Carmen (4109m.) (1 h.).

From the dividing platform abseil down a chimney on the W side and continue down to the Brèche du Diable (4054m. VT). Go up the easy main ridge to reach the Brèche de l'Isolée (4078m. VT) (1 h.). The Isolée lies off the main ridge to the L and can be avoided altogether. It is climbed as follows.

From the gap descend 15m. in a couloir, then traverse a few m. L on to the N face. Climb some cracks (IV) to a little terrace, then take a crack on the L (IV), which has an overhanging nose on the edge of the face to its L, and continue up a few m. to a big undercut flake. Climb the crack on its L for a couple of moves to an overlap, then step L (V, peg up high) on to the edge/ridge. Above take a 3m. crack with capstone to a platform, then easy steep rock for 30m. to the summit (4114m.). Descend from the platform by an abseil ($1\frac{1}{2}$ h.). The hard step L on to the ridge can be avoided by leaving the second crack at a big flake foothold about 6m. below the undercut flake. Now traverse horizontally L just below the overhanging nose (IV). Swing round (IV, exposed, peg) to reach a flake running across the S face. Follow this to a short groove and climb it and a wall above (IV) to the abovementioned platform.

Return to the Brèche de l'Isolée and continue up the main ridge towards the summit. Keep slightly R of the crest up to the foot of the last step. Climb an obvious break, first to the R then back L. Continue easily to the summit (1 h., $6\frac{1}{2}$-$8\frac{1}{2}$ h. from Col du Diable, 11-13 h. from Torino hut).

East (Diable) Couloir. The large gully with a complex exit depression rising between the Diable ridge and the NE face of the mtn. The general gully line bends R towards the summit. At least three main ways have been taken for exits in the upper part. A varied and difficult climb on snow, ice and rock, on the whole steeper at the top and in normal conditions more serious than the Gervasutti couloir. D, 800m. Average angle 49°, getting steeper in the upper sections. The principal objective dangers can be avoided by being well established on the climb by dawn. First ascent: G. Antoldi, G. Boccalatte, R. Chabod, M. Gallo and P. Ghiglione, 31 August, 1930. First winter ascent: H. Agresti and J. Fanton, 9 March, 1968. First solo: R. Chère, 31 July, 1972. Winter solo: M. Batard, 1 January, 1975.

111 The snow slopes under the NE face of the mtn. are roughly midway between the Midi cableway upper station and the Torino hut, about 2h. walking from either starting pt. (Route 28).

Climb crevassed slopes in a glacier bay to the foot of the large snow/ice couloir which appears to descend from the Aigs. du Diable high up to the L (30 min.). Cross the bergschrund under the avalanche cone and climb trending L until the couloir narrows distinctly. Now take steep rocks up the L side for c. 70m. to above the narrowing. Continue straight up at first then trend R but keeping to the L side of the couloir slope. Continue thus past the level of the base of the Diable pillar on the R side of the couloir (3843m. VT), the top of which is a distinct tower (4067m.). The couloir now commences to bend R. Make a long rising traverse R, latterly over rock above the R branch of the couloir, to a rib which divides the upper section from a pt. about 100m. above the base of the Diable pillar. The couloir can also be crossed at a lower level to the foot of the Diable pillar, followed by a direct ascent then a traverse L across the base of the R branch to join the rib. Climb this rib first up a short crack (IV) then mixed ground for some distance to finish by two pitches of IV where the rib joins the SE (Diable) ridge in its topmost section, about 2/3rds way between the Brèche de l'Isolée and the summit (Route 110) (6-9 h. from bergschrund).

L-hand branch exit to Brèche de l'Isolée. M. Marty with J. Théron, 11 July, 1956. Instead of making the long traverse R to the upper rib, at a suitable pt. in the couloir continue up its main snow/ice slope to the saddle adjoining the Isolée on the Diable ridge, then as for Route 110 to the top (5 h. from bergschrund to ridge, 1 h. more to summit).

Note: The R-hand branch has been climbed by a difficult route slanting L across the lower part of the Diable pillar and up to the gap behind the pillar, where the route on the latter is joined.

North-East Face

112 Diable Pillar. A complex route approaching by a steeply rising traverse above the R side of the Diable couloir across the lower sections of other pillars forming the L side of the NE face. Once reached the pillar itself gives a series of sustained pitches, V/V+ and A1, with a narrow connecting rock ridge over a saddle to the terminal summit pillar. First ascent: E. Cavalieri, P. Ravaioni, E. and G. L. Vaccari, 11-13 August, 1963. In winter: S. Avagnina, G. Comino and A. Nebiolo, 27-28 December, 1975.

113 Three Points Pillar (3855m. VT). This large acicular buttress flanks the R side of the Diable couloir below the Diable pillar proper. Its isolated summit stands 125m. above the gap which it forms with the next buttress (the Nameless pillar) rising up the face towards the Diable pillar. Thus there is no natural continuation up the mtn. It has been climbed by two fine routes and variations, TD+/ED, on the L and R edges of the outer face, the former first by E. Cavalieri, A. Mellano, R. Perego and B. Tron, 13-14 August, 1959. The ascent routes are normally reversed by abseiling. However, in 1973 MM. Challéat, Ramouillet and Colaer climbed the pillar by a new variation, abseiled off the top into the gap and continued by a line turning the Nameless pillar to reach the top part of the Gervasutti pillar and thus the top of the mtn. ED.

114 Super Couloir. The jargonistic and probably unapproved name given to the long (800m.) and deeply encased narrow couloir between the Three Points and Gervasutti pillars. A very severe and hazardous expedition with considerable technical difficulties on rock and ice. ED. First ascent: J. M. Boivin and P. Gabarrou, 18-20 May, 1975.

Gervasutti Pillar. The narrow pillar situated between the Three Points pillar (L) and the Central (Boccalatte) pillar (R), the latter descending in a lower splayed out buttress to form the lowest pt. of the face. Arguably the most important route on the face, it is certainly one of the finest rock climbs in the range. The pillar is named after Giusto Gervasutti who died attempting its first ascent in 1946. The lower part of the climb has sustained difficulties and the outcome depends on a long tricky traverse near the top. Rock generally excellent. Harder than the Boccalatte pillar. TD with pitches of V+ and VI, alternatives of A1/2. 800m. First ascent: P. Fornelli and G. Mauro, 29-30 July, 1951. First winter ascent: D. Rabbi and G. Ribaldone, 27 February - 2 March, 1965. First British ascent: M. Boysen and N. J. Estcourt, 12-13 July, 1967. First solo: G. P. Motti, 15 July, 1969 (solo by N. Jaeger, 1974, in $4\frac{1}{2}$ h.). Climbed more than 50 times at end of 1975.

115 Start from the glacier bay below the Diable couloir (Route 111). Climb R over a bergschrund to the foot of a narrow snow/ice gully running up R to the small gap at the top of the lower spur supporting the central pillar. The Gervasutti pillar commences immediately at a rock toe on the L side of this gully. Start just R of the toe and take a diagonal crack leading up to the pillar edge (30m., V, pegs). Continue up a shallow groove and exit L to a good ledge (V). Climb a lay-back crack directly (6m., IV) then traverse L (V) to easier rock. Go up this diagonally R to the foot of the steep central section of the pillar. Start just R of the crest, climb a groove for 25m. (IV) then traverse L to the crest line. Climb a crack direct (IV+) and go through a hole behind a block to a small roof. Surmount this direct (V+ or A1) to reach a horizontal crack and pull up the L edge of the wall above using a peg hold (VI or V and A1 with more pegs). A slightly easier variation to this pitch has been made to the L.

Above is a large yellow tower with an obvious crack line on its L. Climb the crack for 10m. (IV) then traverse easily R on to the pillar edge and continue directly to a platform (40m., exposed, V+). The next section can be varied. Either take an easy groove for 30m. on the R of a large red roof, then a 10m. crack (A2) to a ledge above the roof. Or, traverse horizontally L for 3m. (V) to enter a small groove, climb its back for 20m. (V) up to the roof, then step L for 2m. and pull up overhanging flakes to the ledge above (V+). From here traverse delicately L to a chimney, climb to its top (IV+) then continue up a short crest to a small gap.

Climb a chimney line on the L of the pillar for 70m. with varied pitches of III, IV and V to a large terrace. On the R of the crest climb a short wall, some blocks then a groove (10m., V) which returns to the crest. From the centre of an icy ramp about 6m. R, ascend to a vertical crack and take this to another ledge (A1/2). (This pitch can be turned further R by hard free climbing). Climb another crack on the R (V) to reach the foot of the final step on the pillar proper. Follow a long diagonal ramp line R, normally very icy and delicate with poor protection and loose rock, finishing up a crack (20m., IV+) to a small col.

Continue by a 20m. chimney then easy rock to a little shoulder near the foot of two towers separated by a narrow chimney. Descend a small gully L to the foot of the chimney. Traverse a few m. L and climb a chimney on the L of the second tower (IV, icy). Avoid the tower easily and reach the gap at the foot of a large red tower. Junction with Boccalatte pillar. Ascend L of the tower in a small couloir between two ribs then climb broken rocks to the saddle at the top of the tower. Continue up the ridge, turning pinnacles on the R side, to a grey tower about 30m. high. Climb this direct (IV/IV+) then descend a little to an upper snow slope leading to the summit (9-13 h. from foot).

Boccalatte (Central) Pillar. This pillar runs up the centre of the NE face but is less pronounced than the Gervasutti pillar to its L. It rises above a lower buttress descending to mark the lowest rock toe of the face (3281m. VT). The gap at the top of this buttress marks the access pt. to the Boccalatte route. A natural line and a good route with variations adopted according to conditions. Rock generally excellent. By the easiest combination in good conditions, D/D+ with pitches of III and IV. Snowed up rock and generally icy conditions will force a party to take to more open rock pitches of V/V+. The direct finish by the Red Tower is V+, sustained. Climbed less often than the Gervasutti pillar. 800m. First ascent: Nina Pietrasanta and G. Boccalatte, 28 August, 1936. Direct finish by Red Tower: R. Michon del Campo with G. Rébuffat, 7 August, 1946. First winter ascent: E. Chrobak, M. Marchal and M. Schneider, 25-26 March, 1967 (earlier winter season ascents made in the 1970s). First British ascent: B. Hall and J. Whittle, March, 1975 (climbed by an Englishman in a continental party, 1972).

116 Start exactly as for the Gervasutti pillar (Route 115). At the foot of the couloir running up to the gap at the top of the lower buttress, move a little R and climb a secondary slabby gully (IV) until loose broken rocks can be followed L into the main couloir of snow/rocks which is climbed to the gap. Traverse diagonally R over snowy rocks below the main pillar to its vaguely defined R edge. Climb the R side of this until it develops steeply above, then traverse 20m. L across it into a couloir running parallel with the main edge. Go up this couloir for several pitches on steep snowy slabs, delicate with technical pitches of III which become hard in anything less than perfect conditions, up to a snowy shoulder. To the L of the couloir and near its top the 200m. high Tour Carrée rises as a continuation of the pillar.

An alternative to this couloir section is to take the pillar edge direct. This gives superb climbing with pitches of IV, V and V+ up to the vertical summit step of the lower pillar. The latter is turned on the L by the aforesaid couloir, by its top section which is still delicate, to return R at the snowy shoulder.

Now climb the R flank of the pillar for about 80m. on steep and usually icy rocks normally constituting the most trying part of the ascent, delicate with poor protection, then return L to the crest, now above the Tour Carrée and another small tower, and keeping L reach a little higher the gap under the Red Tower. This is above a lower gap and another tower bypassed by the 80m. section. Junction with Gervasutti pillar. Continue by Route 115 to the top (6-12 h. from bergschrund).

Direct finish by Red Tower. From the gap traverse R for 10m. to icy grooves. Climb these (V+) then slant L to a small snowy shoulder. Continue trending R for 20m. to a large groove. Climb this by its slabby walls and crack (20m., V+) to two slanting dièdres on the R. Take the R-hand one (V) to the crest of the tower, good stance. Continue direct by a slab (V) and a crack line (V+), and exit R just below the top of the tower. Move L to reach a saddle behind the tower where Route 115 is joined.

117 Central Pillar Direct. The line of the true edge of the Boccalatte pillar (q.v.) actually descends to the R of the lower buttress forming a toe in the glacier. The first gap reached by the normal approach to the Boccalatte pillar can also be reached from the opposite R side up a very steep rib on mixed ground and hard rock. This rib is the "direct" start. The pillar edge is then climbed direct to where the Boccalatte route traverses L into the top part of the couloir flanking the lower pillar section. From here an abseil is taken to the foot of the Tour Carrée further L. This great tower then a smaller one are climbed direct to the base of the Red Tower where the Boccalatte route is joined again. ED with pitches of VI. First ascent: J. Coquegniot and F. Guillot, 1 July, 1968 (in 12 h. from bergschrund to summit of mtn.). Solo and second ascent: N. Jaeger, 20 July, 1975 in $4\frac{1}{2}$ h.).

MT. BLANC DU TACUL NE face

L'Isolée

4067
Diable
pillar

Red Tower

110

120 Tour
Carrée

3955

121

Quille
pillar

111

3843

Super couloir

3 pts pillar

Gervasutti pillar

Gervasutti couloir

116

Escargots pillar

Gervasutti couloir

115

Quille couloir

121

Jager couloir

NE Face
Annexe

121

120

Diable couloir

114

Pyramide

3281

127

118 <u>Quille Couloir.</u> The long ice gully between the Boccalatte pillar (L) and Quille pillar (R). Steeper and harder than the Diable and Gervasutti couloirs. Considerable stonefall danger. TD. First ascent (solo): B. Macho, 16 May, 1973. The lower part of the couloir then an independent line to the R to reach the NE spur near the summit was climbed by R. Barton and R. Shaw, 28-30 December, 1973.

119 <u>Quille Pillar.</u> The Quille is a rock finger jutting out from the top of a large rock buttress coming down from near pt. 3955m. on the L side of the NE pillar of the face. The pillar/buttress occupies the middle section of this part of the face. It is flanked to the L by the big Quille couloir, by which the base of the pillar is reached, and which itself divides the couloir into two distinct branches in its lower part. The route follows the L edge of the pillar/buttress up to the top of the Quille, which is detached from the NE pillar. Two abseils off the top and a rising traverse on the L side are made to join the NE pillar near the top of the mtn. Scenically and technically a fine mixed route, unfortunately marred by serious stonefall danger until the foot of the pillar proper is reached. TD with pitches of V and A2. 40 pegs. 17 h. First ascent: D. Mollaret and Y. Seigneur, 3-4 April, 1965. First winter ascent: J. C. Droyer and J. F. Pommaret, 25-26 February, 1975.

<u>North-East Pillar/Spur.</u> The large ridge at the R side of the face which borders the Gervasutti couloir. A big gendarme high on the ridge just above the detached finger summit of the Quille pillar is marked pt. 3955m. A splendid mixed climb, D+ with pitches of V/V+. First ascent: C. Aureli, E. Cavalieri, E. Montagna and S. Sironi, 11-12 August, 1965.

120 On the glacier at the foot of the face climb towards the base of the Gervasutti couloir. Cross the bergschrund about

75m. further L and climb a short ice slope to below a small rock/snow couloir leading R to the crest of the pillar. The lowest pt. of the pillar is still further down to the L. Climb easy rocks L of the couloir and trend R up slabs for 30m. (III and IV) into the couloir and go up it to a small gap in the crest. Follow the ridge to below a steep gendarme. Now traverse 70m. horizontally R then return obliquely L by steep and exposed climbing to the crest at the foot of another gendarme. Turn this on the R by icy slabs and rejoin the crest above. Continue up the steep crest by a short delicate section on snow/ice then a slab section to mixed icy ground. From the uppermost slab climb steep ice trending L for 40m. to a snowy terrace at the foot of smooth walls. Ascend a few m. L to a crack and climb this (4m., V) to a sloping terrace. From here make a hard move L to reach another smooth, strenuous crack and take this (8m., V) to a niche below the overhang closing the crack. Turn this L by a slanting crack and mantelshelf on to a small ledge (5m., V+). To the L take a short wall (IV+) and continue straight up (30m. IV+) to the top of the buttress. One is now above the top of the Quille pillar to the L.

Continue along the crest to the foot of a notable gendarme (3955m.). Partly climb this then turn its top on the L side over grey rock, finishing with a delicate traverse (IV) to rejoin the crest above the gap behind the gendarme. After a slope of loose mixed ground the spur, always bending L, is followed as directly as possible with short variable obstacles up to a terminal ice slope which leads to the top of the mtn. (14 h. from bergschrund on first ascent).

Gervasutti (North- East) Couloir. The prominent snow/ice couloir bordering the R (N) side of the central section of the NE face. It broadens at the top and is closed by a large sérac band which is avoided by the two main exits, L (direct) and R (normal). On its R lies a continuation face of lesser rock spurs which for the purposes of this guide is called the NE face Annexe (see below). This couloir is generally more serious than all the famous eponymous gullies now climbed frequently in the range, e.g. Spencer, Whymper, Couturier, etc., on account of its steepness and potential objective danger. The slope starts at 45°, soon reaching 50° in the middle and 55° for some distance under the séracs. Steeper sections occur along the edges where the couloir is normally climbed. The route is very exposed to falling stones and ice and is best done at night in cold weather. It is distinctly safer in the winter season when it has been done frequently in recent times. Nearly all parties take the easier R-hand exit which is less dangerous. A classic and popular ice route of high technical and scenic interest, climbed over 200 times (50 in winter) to date. D-/D. The L-hand exit must be rated D+. 800m. The original ascent of the couloir abandoned the slope less than halfway up and took the R-hand enclosing spur to the top. Rarely repeated. P. Filippi, P. Ghiglione and F. Ravelli, 1 September, 1929.

L-hand (direct) exit - First ascent: R. Chabod and G. Gervasutti, 13 August, 1934. No record traced of winter ascent by this exit.

R-hand (normal) exit - First ascent: L. Lachenal and L. Terray, May, 1948. In winter: A. Marchionni, L. Mazzaniga, A. Mellano, R. Perego, G. Ribaldone and A. Risso, 25 February, 1962 (18 days previously another party had climbed to the exit cornice and descended the same route). First solo: Hermann Buhl, 19 August, 1956 in $1\frac{1}{2}$ h. Solo in winter: J. P. Ollagnier, 1973. First British ascent: M. Burke and D. Haston, 1 February, 1967. Solo by Eric Jones, 1970. Descended on ski by S. Saudan, 16 October, 1968 in 40 min. ($1\frac{1}{2}$ h. from summit of mtn.).

121 Reach the gentle glacier slopes below the couloir at a pt. roughly midway between the Midi cableway upper station and the Torino hut, about 2 h. walking from either starting pt. (Route 28).

Cross the bergschrund at the obvious avalanche cone (c. 3460m.) and climb straight up the L side of the couloir on runnelled snow/ice of gradually increasing steepness to below the sérac band and about level with the Quille tower or the gendarme just above it on the spur to the L. The couloir broadens and steepens again.

L-hand exit. Make an ascending traverse L on a steep line and get on to a similarly steep whale-back snow/ice crest running up to the L-hand end of the ice wall. Take the easiest line L of the wall, normally with two or three hard ice pitches, to join another steep slope soon easing off and leading directly to the summit (8-9 h. from bergschrund).

R-hand exit. Make an ascending traverse R and reach a bordering snowy rock rib on this side. Either climb beside it or on it, according to conditions, and go through a cornice at the top near pt. 4130. Return L-wards up an easy snow slope above the top of the couloir to reach the summit (6-8 h. from bergschrund).

North-East Face Annexe

A series of steep rock spurs extending R-wards from the Gervasutti couloir, finishing along the top of the N then NE ridge of the mtn. and decreasing in height towards the R (N). Several routes have been made in this area.

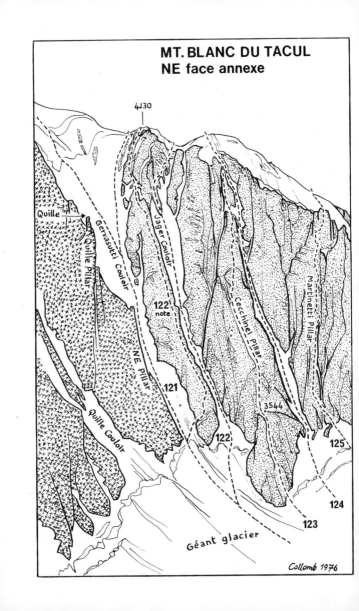

MT. BLANC DU TACUL
NE face annexe

Collomb 1976

122 <u>Jager Couloir.</u>   The first couloir R of the Gervasutti
couloir, separated from the latter by a long, narrow low relief
spur.   (The spur was first climbed complete by Y. Charlet
and G. Parrau, 7 January, 1975 - no special interest).   It is
much narrower and perhaps steeper than its famous neighbour.
D.   600m.   First ascent: P. Barthélémy and C. Jager, 12
June, 1964.   First winter ascent (solo):   W. Cecchinel,
17 January, 1971.

123 <u>Cecchinel Pillar.</u> The obvious spur R of the Jager couloir,
descending furthest into the glacier slope.   The top of its first
step is pt. 3544.   A mixed climb with some loose sections and
a fine slender tower of 80m. on excellent granite in the upper
part. 650m. TD. First ascent: W. Cecchinel and C. Daubas,
11 August, 1973.

124 <u>Couloir between Cecchinel and Martinetti Pillars.</u>   A very
serious climb with hard ice bulges in the narrows at mid-height
and an exit on steep mixed ground.   ED/ED+.   First ascent:
J. P. Albinoni and P. Gabarrou during night of 4-5 July, 1974
(9 h.).

125 <u>Martinetti Pillar.</u>   The third pillar to the R of the Gervasutti couloir, starting above and R of the base of the larger
Cecchinel pillar, and marked at the top by a large red tower.
Probably the most worthwhile route on the Annexe, being
steeper, cleaner, on good rock and more continuous than the
other spurs.   TD+ with pitches of VI.   30 pegs and wedges.
500m.   Photo diagram in La Montagne 1960, p. 292.   First
ascent: M. Martinetti and C. Mollier, 23 August, 1960.
Repeated in 1962.

North Face Facet

Half a dozen routes have been made on this relatively small triangular facet which stands directly above and S of the broad plateau of the Col du Midi, opposite the cableway station. Its summit is marked pt. 3970. A large glacier tongue to its L borders the NE ridge of the mtn. Most of the routes are rated AD but they are serious and sustained of their kind and are not ideal alternatives for descending to the Col du Midi in the event of slopes or bergschrunds on the normal route becoming dangerous to negotiate. See remarks in preamble to the mtn. itself.

North Face Facet, Left-Hand Ridge.

The rock spur descending lowest to the L of the central depression in the facet. Probably the easiest route and one taken several times in descent as an alternative to the normal route on to the Col du Midi. A fine little climb of 350m. on mixed terrain. AD. First ascent: G. Gren, G. Grisolle, A. Poulain and M. Ziegler with A. Contamine, 4 July, 1968.

126 From the Col du Midi (3532m.) cross the snow plateau to the base of the ridge. Cross a bergschrund to the L and climb L of the rocks on steep snow/ice into a broad couloir leading R to a little saddle at the top of the first continuous rock section of the ridge. From the saddle climb an overhanging rock band (not difficult in good conditions), trending L and continue up the broad line of the ridge to an ice slope. Climb this to a narrow ice couloir on the L side of the steep headwall. Follow the couloir to the ridge of the headwall which leads to the top of the facet (3-4 h.). Continue up the N ridge of the mtn. first on moderately steep snow slopes, then at an easy angle, keeping slightly R with big cornices on L (1 h., 4-5 h. from Col du Midi).

Satellites of Mont Blanc du Tacul

The NE ridge of the mtn., a major branch of the N ridge, terminates in Pte. Lachenal. All the other outliers appear below the Aigs. du Diable ridge.

Below the Col du Diable the Aigs. du Diable ridge descends slightly to two prominent points - the Aiguillettes du Tacul (3913m. and 3901m.). From the Aiguillettes the ridge divides into two main branches, separated by a prominent snow couloir - the Couloir des Aiguillettes. The first branch goes down to the Grand Capucin, the Petit Capucin and Pte. Adolphe Rey. The second branch goes down to the Clocher, the Petit Clocher and the Trident. A small secondary ridge goes down to the Chandelle.

Further N from the groupings developed below the Aiguillettes are the isolated rock masses of the Chat and Pyramide. The appendage "du Tacul" to several pts. among the satellites is dropped to avoid confusion with identically named outliers of the Aig. du Tacul on the opposite (E) side of the Géant glacier basin.

POINTE LACHENAL   3613m.

The last significant point on the NW ridge of the mtn. before the Col du Gros Rognon. Its SE face is only a few hundred m. distance across a glacier bay from the NE Face Annexe of the mtn. The face is 250m. high and gives a number of climbs on excellent rock of the same quality as those on the SE face of the Aig. du Midi. Standard throughout, V/V+ and A1/2. From L to R within a short distance of each other: SSE Buttress (Fréchin, Martinetti, 1960), SE Face (Cecchinel, Jager, 1968), SE Buttress (Labrunie, Wohlschlag, Contamine, 1959). The last is quite popular and takes the L side of the buttress, well marked by pegs in place.

PYRAMIDE (DU TACUL)   3468m.

An isolated rock buttress midway between the foot of Pte. Adolphe Rey and the main NE face of the mtn. Numerous interesting, short but stiff rock climbs generally grade V or harder. A new route was put up as recently as 1975. First ascent (by NNW ridge, III): R. Chabod and M. Mila, 2 July, 1934. First British ascent: G. G. MacPhee with A. Ottoz, 1949.

East Ridge. A short, interesting training climb on good rock, done frequently. 270m., pitches of IV/IV+. First ascent: E. Croux, L. Grivel and A. Ottoz, 29 July, 1940.

127 The foot of the buttress is reached from the Torino hut or Midi cableway station by glacier walking in 1½-2 h. (Route 28). Start on the L-hand side of the lowest pt. and climb ledges and steps to the crest of the ridge. Follow this fairly easily for 30m. to a steep wall. Turn this on the L by a smooth slab (IV) then take a short groove (IV) and easier rocks to rejoin the crest. A little higher climb a crack up a wall, L then R, for 20m. (IV) to a roof of large blocks. Climb the L side of the overhang, delicate (IV+, peg) followed by a short crack (IV+) to a good stance. Behind, go up a steep grey slab (III-), then take a vertical chimney/crack on the R which slants L with chockstones (IV) to the slabby crest line. Take more steep slabs on the R side of the ridge (III, IV). Return to the crest about 40m. from the summit which is soon reached. When the upper slabs are wet or icy there is a hard groove on the L side of the ridge leading to the last easy crest (2-3 h. from foot).

128 Descent: Either make 2 or 3 easy abseils down the N(NNW) ridge to a snow crest halfway up the L side of the snow slope between the Pyramide and the Chat, then descend the short steep slope in a few min., with one or two bergschrunds, generally not serious, to the glacier slopes below (45 min., roughly line of original first ascent). Or (normal), descend 60m. distance down the E ridge, then slant L down terraces from where 2 or 3 abseils straight down the N face lead to a snow slope and the glacier (45 min.). Or, make 3 fine abseils, not exactly in line but straightforward, down the 100m. high W side to the snow col between the Pyramide and the Chat, then descend the snow slopes, short but steep at the top, on the N side (45 min. - 1 h.).

LE CHAT   3500m.

A rock tower behind the Pyramide with a characteristic jutting summit chin.   No special interest, very difficult to climb, grade VI without artificial techniques. First ascent: L. Grivel and A. Ottoz, 29 July, 1940.

POINTE ADOLPHE REY   3536m.

The detached terminal buttress of the Capucin ridge, a splendid training ground affording quality rock climbs, some of which are serious undertakings in their own right.   Most of the routes are of a high technical standard. First ascent: Nina Pietrasanta, G. Boccalatte, R. Chabod and G. Gervasutti, 16 July, 1935.

West Ridge and North Face.   A short but serious climb, advisable only in dry conditions. IV/IV+. First ascensionists.

129 From the Torino hut follow Route 23 as far as the foot of the Tour Ronde.   Cross the glacier NW to the foot of the couloir descending from the gap (3362m. VT) between Pte. Adolphe Rey and the Petit Capucin.   Reach the gap by steep broken rocks on the R side of the couloir (2 h.).   Go up the easy initial part of the W ridge to the foot of a smooth vertical step.   Traverse L a short way on to the N face, then abseil 12m. into the bottom of a little ice-glazed couloir. Climb 4m. L to a block platform detached from the face. Climb a thin crack in the vertical wall above for c.15m., then traverse horizontally L (2 pegs) across a vague rib to a large projecting block. Climb vertical rock above trending R for 30m., then take a short slab on the R and traverse 15m. L over friable rocks to a short chimney. Above this reach a shoulder on the E ridge and climb a short vertical step then a final easy ridge to the summit ($1\frac{1}{2}$ h., $3\frac{1}{2}$ h. from Torino hut).

130 Descent down NW ridge to gap. Make 3 abseils down the ridge, first on the crest then just R of it to the terrace where the original N face route traverses L. A further short abseil leads to easy rock and the gap.

<u>North-East Ridge</u>. One of the best routes on the buttress with continuously difficult free climbing in the lower section. Several variations have been made. V/V+, 350m. The lower half of the ridge consists of two prominent buttresses divided by a huge groove. The lower R-hand one provides the route. First ascent: R. Guillaume and L. Terray, 15 September, 1958.

131 From the Torino hut reach the base and lowest pt. of the ridge from Route 28 ($1\frac{1}{2}$ h.). At the bottom is a short wall. Start R of this and climb 30m. up an obvious break filled with loose rock to an overhang. Traverse R to the crest of a small rib and follow this for 4m. (V+), then climb L using a diagonal crack (V+ without peg) to above the overhang. Now climb a 10m. groove R of a small rock beak, then follow grooves of red rock for 50m. before moving L to go up a grey crack system (IV) to a prominent overhang. Continue straight up the L-hand side of the overhang then descend a broken chimney, peg in place, down to the L for 10m. From here reach the main ridge crest in a few steps and move L into an obvious groove which is climbed to the crest and another short pitch before a vertical section on the crest.

On the L take a chimney/crack for a few m. (pegs) then

traverse R up a toe line (V) on to the R side of the crest and take another chimney/crack for a few moves (V, pegs) to a small ledge. Continue the strenuous chimney/crack for a few m. and avoid.a small roof on the R (V+, pegs) to arrive below a larger roof. Make a difficult rope move L (V+) to a crack leading to an overhang. Go over this (5 pegs) and another overhang (IV+, pegs) into a steep groove climbed on better holds (IV) to a good stance. Above, climb R across a wall (V) and go up steep cracks (V, peg) to a detached block. Pull up on to the crest and follow it more easily to a large platform where the two lower buttresses of the ridge merge.

Climb diagonally L (IV) to a small gap below a large tower. Now move on to the R-hand (N) face, traversing and rising up short steep wall pitches (IV+) to reach the gap behind the tower. From the gap descend 2m. on the L (S) side and traverse L along a delicate ledge to a groove. Climb this (V, pegs) then easier slabs to rejoin the ridge which is followed over a few short steps to the top (5-7 h. from foot).

132 <u>East-South-East Spur (Salluard Route).</u> This spur is the L-hand one of the two referred to in the previous route. It starts from the head of a short steep crevassed slope. The most frequented climb on the peak. 300m., V with 30 pegs and wedges. The route keeps generally L of the spur crest till it reaches the large gendarme where Route 131 is joined. No communicated details. There is a fairly full description in the Vallot guide and a verbatim translation of it in the Rébuffat Mt. Blanc book. First ascent: T. Busi with F. Salluard, 6 September, 1951. In winter: G. Rabbi and G. Rossi, 1958.

PETIT CAPUCIN 3693m.

A fairly frequented secondary rock pt. on the ridge rising

from Pte. Adolphe Rey to the Grand Capucin. A large gendarme on the SE side/ridge is the Roi de Siam (3632m. VT). First ascent: L. de Riseis with A. and H. Rey, 25 August, 1914.

West Ridge (from Brèche du Carabinier). The ordinary and descent route. PD. Steep snow and solid rock scrambling. First ascensionists.

133 From the Torino hut follow Route 23 as far as the foot of the Tour Ronde. Cross the glacier NW to the foot of the couloir descending from the gap between the Petit and Grand Capucin. This couloir adjoins the larger Aiguillettes couloir rising L. The gap is the Brèche du Carabinier, divided in two by the Carabinier monolith (3612m. VT). The R-hand (NE) opening is on the Petit Capucin side.

Cross a sometimes awkward bergschrund (2 h.) and climb snow/ice and rocks to the R-hand gap. Continue up the W ridge on good rocks to the summit ($1\frac{1}{4}$ h., $3\frac{1}{4}$ h. from Torino hut).

East Face. An excellent, classic training climb of 250 m., IV with a pitch of V. First ascent: C. Arnoldi, G. Gagliardone and G. Gervasutti, 16 August, 1946. First British ascent: R. G. Collomb and R. S. Mowll, 22 July, 1955.

134 From the Torino hut or Midi cableway station approach as for Route 129 to the gap between Pte. Adolphe Rey and the Petit Capucin ($2-2\frac{1}{2}$ h.). PD. Go down a few m. on the other side of the gap and traverse R (N) across a couloir and over steep icy rocks for 60m. to below the narrow facet of the E face. From an upper terrace climb an initial wall by a crack (III) to a good ledge below a chockstone chimney on the R. Take the chimney (25m., V, pegs, strenuous), then trend L up a short wall and return R to a series of parallel cracks and grooves which are climbed for 30m. (IV/IV+) to a stance.

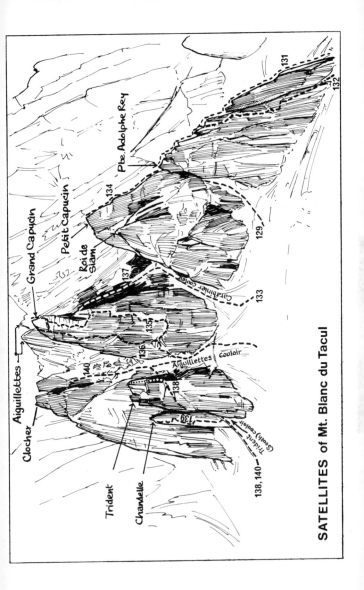

Clocker
Aiguillettes
Grand Capucin
Petit Capucin
Roi de Siam
Pte. Adolphe Rey
Trident
Chandelle
Carabinier Couloir
Aiguillettes Couloir
Trident (South) couloir

129
131
132
133
134
135
136
137
138
139
140
138, 140

SATELLITES of Mt. Blanc du Tacul

Above, an easier groove (IV-) leads in 30m. to an obvious block at the foot of a large red wall. Climb the slabby wall by a crack line on the L (IV-) with a steep finish. Continue trending R and climb by short cracks (III) to the last pitch. Go up this by a crack slanting L (IV-) to the summit (3 h., 5-5½ h. from Torino hut).

GRAND CAPUCIN 3838m.

The most impressive pinnacle of this satellite group and probably the most famous granite monolith in the range. It is now essentially a practice ground for serious artificial climbing but the summit itself is a worthy mountaineering objective. Completely artificial routes on the S and N sides are omitted. First ascent: E. Augusto with A. and H. Rey and L. Lanier, 24 July, 1924.

First ascensionists route on West side. This is only of historical interest, being climbed originally by unorthodox artificial means. About 80m. By modern methods rated V with a pitch of VI and two pitches of A1. The modern descent route (see below) approximates to the line.

East Face (Original Bonatti Route). An impressive and very enjoyable route for addicts of aid climbing. Almost entirely artificial, sustained and strenuous. Easily the most classic route of this style in the range. The first ascent took four days and the party used about 160 pegs/wedges. Nowadays a fast party can avoid a bivouac. There are normally 200-250 pegs, etc. in place, but depegging by certain guides occurs from time to time. Care should be taken when using old wedges and other gear left in place. Climbed relatively cleanly, with 40 pegs: VI and A1. Normally, with four or more times this number of pegs/wedges: V, with a great deal of A1/2. 420m.

First ascent: Walter Bonatti and Luciano Ghigo, 20-23 July,

1951. First British ascent: T. D. Bourdillon and H. G. Nicol, 1952. First winter ascent: G. Alippi, R. Merendi and L. Tenderini, 27 February - 1 March, 1959. First solo: Gino Buscaini, 23-25 June, 1959.

135 From the Torino hut follow Route 133 into the Aiguillettes couloir ($1\frac{1}{2}$ h.). Cross a bergschrund and climb the first 100m. of the couloir on the L of the face, then trend R up broken rocks, sometimes icy, to reach the L-hand end of terraces which cross the lower part of the face. Cross the terraces to the R-hand end and descend easy ledges and short chimneys to the foot of a smooth red slab. Climb diagonally R across the slab (V) for 10m. to a small ledge and descend using the rope to another ledge. Walk along this ledge past a good cave (bivouac site) to the foot of two grooves. Climb the R-hand groove for 10m. (A1) then go up easily for 5m. to a good ledge on the R. Follow this L for a few m. (V) and climb over jammed blocks to a big flake. Climb the groove above (V, A1) and traverse 5m. L to a good stance. Climb the chimney above (V) to a pinnacle then take the groove above for about 30m. until it gives out on to a smooth slab topped by an enormous overhang (A1/2, V, stance in étriers). Take the lower of two possible traverse lines for 10m. (V) into a deep-cut groove and follow this (A1, V) to a good ledge on the R of the overhang (first Bonatti bivouac).

Climb the grooves above for 12m. (V, A1) then move 3m. R to a very narrow ledge. Climb the narrow groove above to an overhang and go over this (A2) to a small stance. Leave the main groove and traverse horizontally R (A1) to a chimney and climb this (IV) to a good ledge on top of a flake. Above is the 40m. Wall, possibly the hardest section of the climb; two long pitches and a stance in étriers. Start over a small overhang and follow the line of pegs trending to the R up a thin crack and a shallow overhanging groove. Move R and up a cracked wall to an excellent ledge, usually with water or snow,

191

on the edge of the N face (second Bonatti bivouac).

Traverse L along an easy ledge, climb a 3m. wall and continue the traverse to the end of a second ledge. Step L and climb a steep groove for 22m. below a large roof. Climb the roof direct (A2 or VI) and take the steep crack above to another overhang (A2). Traverse 10m. R to a small ledge and go straight up a crack (V, A1) to the second of two small niches (third Bonatti bivouac).

Go up to the overhang above and traverse 3m. L into a groove. Climb the groove (A1) to a stance in étriers on the L. Continue up a crack in the slab above (A1) and traverse L to a good stance. Climb a vertical crack (A2) and move R up slabs to a bulge (V+ or A1). Take the L-hand crack to a good stance below the enormous summit overhang (IV and A1). Climb a groove and slab on the R to the NE ridge (V). Descend a little and traverse on the N face (IV), then go up a groove (IV+) to snowy ledges giving access to the summit (10-12 h. for face).

East Face Direct. This route is nearly all artificial, with about 150 pegs, 10 bolts and 25 wedges. Pitches of VI, A3. 400m. It takes a line L of the Bonatti and R of the Swiss route on the S face. First ascent: A. Anghileri, G. Cariboni, C. Ferrari, C. Mauri and P. Negri, 29-30 June and 1 July, 1968. First winter ascent: A. Gogna and T. Cerruti, 9-11 March, 1969.

136 Start from the terraces used to traverse across the face on the previous route. Instead of traversing R, climb for two pitches to reach the highest terrace (IV). From this upper pt. climb a vertical, well defined crack on the L (VI, 12 pegs, 4 wedges) for 40m. Now go immediately R for 3m. (peg) then free climb delicately up R, to a crack (peg). Climb this to a good ledge (VI, 2 pegs).

Traverse 15m. R and reach a huge dièdre. Climb directly over an overhang (VI, A3, 15 pegs) and belay after 20m. Climb 20m. further, then leave the main dièdre by a crack in its R side. Climb this past a terrace to a second terrace (VI, 15 pegs, bolt, 4 wedges). Bivouac on first ascent.

Alternative: From just below the overhang in the main dièdre pegs lead up steeply R to reach the bivouac ledge (previous attempt).

From the bivouac ledge, climb an obvious dièdre for 40m. (VI, 25 pegs, 8 wedges). Continue by a crack in its R wall (15m.) then two overhangs (10m.) and finally a dièdre (15m.) to a belay in étriers. Continue up the crack, which borders a blank red wall, for 25m., then cross over to the R for 10m. (VI, 25 pegs, 2 wedges).

Zigzag up the obvious cracks which cut through the over-hangs above for 40m. to a stance (VI, 15 pegs, 2 wedges). After a strenuous 10m. dièdre (4 wedges), climb 30m. up an easier couloir (IV, V). Several possible bivouac places here. Continue up the couloir/dièdre for 30m. The rock overhangs but the pegging is straightforward (VI, 20 pegs). A final 10m. of free climbing leads to the summit. At least one bivouac will be necessary.

137 Descent. This is serious and is dangerous in adverse conditions. Equates to D. Easy rock steps/ledges on the W side under the summit lead down in a few m. to a good rock belay draped with slings. Abseil about 20m. down a steep smooth slab, trending somewhat L (facing in) towards the N wall. So reach a second belay and slings on a comfortable ledge. From here make a partly free abseil direct to a thin snow crest in 40m. This crest leads down in a few m. to the Brèche du Grand Capucin (3760m. VT). From the gap descend the steep ice couloir on the E side towards the Carabinier monolith on the ridge to the L of the couloir (facing down).

This couloir has fixed pegs and belay pts. at intervals of about 35m. which are sometimes buried under snow/ice. Keep L of the ice, on rock which in any case is rotten and dangerous in dry conditions. Five-six abseils lead under the Carabinier into the more comfortable snow couloir running up to the Brèche du Carabinier (Route 133). Go down the latter and over a bergschrund on to the glacier (2-3 h.).

LE TRIDENT   3639m.

A fine tower at the end of the Clocher ridge, with a prominent forked cummit. It is separated from the Grand Capucin by the Aiguillettes couloir. There are several hard free and artificial routes on this pinnacle. First ascent: Mme A. Damesme, M. Damesme and J. de Lépiney, 13 September, 1919. First winter ascent: Mlle E. Stagni, I. Gamboni, J. Martin and R. Wohlschag, 12 March, 1966.

Original/Normal Route. The original route of the first ascensionists is very fine but is probably not followed in its lower part as often as later variations on the Aiguillettes couloir side of the peak. It starts up the SW flank, partly climbs then crosses the S ridge on to the E face where more recent direct approaches converge, and finally takes a communal line on the E face to the top. The original route is considerably more interesting than the variations. A pitch of V+ if climbed without pegs, otherwise IV with a pitch of IV+. 200m.

138 From the Torino hut approach the foot of the Trident as for Route 133, but go into the S couloir to the L (W) of the peak, which descends from the gap of the Brèche du Trident ($1\frac{1}{2}$ h.). Climb this couloir for about 80m. then transfer to rocks on the R side. Climb these by a series of short cracks and chimneys in steep, terraced walls (III/III+) and near the top trend R to a large balcony which adjoins a shoulder on the S ridge. Move R and climb a diagonal crack (IV) into a dièdre bounded on the R by the S ridge. Follow the dièdre for a pitch until a short horizontal crack (IV) leads R to the ridge. Continue up another crack just L of the ridge, with an overhanging start, and rejoin the crest in 12m. (V+, but normally with pegs in place = IV). Now make a steeply rising traverse up to the R on to the E face with good holds and small ledges (III-) to reach terraces below the upper 80m. wall. Climb the wall first by a fairly large chimney (strenuous, IV) then by wide cracks to a platform about 30m. below the gap between the central prong and S prong (L). Continue up cracks trending R for 12m., then traverse R for 4m. (peg) into a crack. Follow this directly to the central prong (IV+, peg). Descend to the gap and make a short delicate traverse on the E face to reach the S prong ($2\frac{1}{2}$ h., about 4 h. from Torino hut).

Variations: These avoid the original crux on the S ridge, but as that in a pegged up condition is no longer the crux, the variations, converging at the terraces high on the E face, have only the merit of being shorter. They are quicker especially in dry conditions when the lower rocks are free of ice.

(i) Instead of taking to the rocks of the SW side, continue up the S couloir by rocks on its R edge to the Brèche du Trident. Cross the gap and descend slightly by traversing L (E) over steep friable rocks some distance above the Aiguillettes couloir. By a continuous slightly descending movement reach a big sloping terrace, normally snowy. From its upper L corner climb a steep slabby pitch (15m., IV) to the lower terraces of the group on the upper face to your L, where the original route is joined 80m. below the top.

(ii) The snowy terrace of (i) can be reached directly out of the Aiguillettes couloir (from about 80m. up it) by a snow/rock couloir which gives short pitches of III/III+, but can be quite icy in poor conditions.

These variations save 30 min.-1 h. on the total climbing

time.

Descent: The quickest descent is to abseil down the upper 80m. of the E face to the first terraces, then abseil down the pitch of Var. (i) to the snowy terrace. Thereafter further short abseils down Var. (ii) into the Aiguillettes couloir. The latter can be steep and icy before the glacier is reached.

LA CHANDELLE   3561m.

East Face. A striking pinnacle just off the ridge joining the Trident and the Clocher. Its original route is short and difficult with free and artificial climbing similar to the E face of the Grand Capucin. (There is another route on the NNE face). V+, A2. First ascent: R. Gallieni with Walter Bonatti, 3-4 August, 1960. First winter (second) ascent: G. Bertone and R. Pellin, 18-19 January, 1967.   Third and first British ascent: R. Mear and a Dane, 1971.

139 From the Torino hut follow Routes 133, 138 to the foot of the S couloir of the Trident ($1\frac{1}{2}$ h.). Cross the bergschrund of the S couloir and go up for about 25m. On the L start up a 15m. crack which splits the first steep walls of the Chandelle, then make a delicate traverse L to the foot of a groove capped by a large square block. Climb the groove and go straight over the overhang. Continue up the overhanging groove above for 15m. to a good ledge.

From the ledge continue straight up a system of cracks, trending slightly towards the R. Belay in étriers. Continue up the overhanging crack line to another small ledge, about 45m. above the previous one. Climb direct again for a few m. by artificial climbing on vertical rock, then free climb for 45m. on red slabs up to a blank section of the face. Make a long exposed traverse to the L for 30m. to a large ledge underneath the large central overhangs (bivouac site).

Descend 2m. to the L to the foot of an overhanging crack and climb this for 20m. This is the hardest pitch of the climb, pegs for aid. Continue up a series of cracks in the middle of smooth walls until about 30m. below the summit. Traverse L for several m. and climb a final difficult crack to the top (22 h. on first ascent).

Descent: Make an impressive free abseil of 40m. to the small col between the Chandelle and the Clocher. Then four long abseils down the N face to the S couloir of the Trident, about 100m. above the starting point.

LE CLOCHER   3853m.

First ascent: T. de Lépiney, R. Picard and P. Tézenas du Montcel, 19 August, 1926.

<u>South-East Side</u>. This can be approached by climbing all the way up the Aiguillettes couloir (between the Trident and Grand Capucin), as by the first ascensionists, or by going up the S couloir of the Trident to reach the upper part of the former couloir. The second approach is much the best. Mixed climbing with stonefall danger, AD+ with pitches of III/IV.

140 From the Torino hut follow Route 138 and its Var. (i) up the S couloir of the Trident to the Brèche du Trident ($2\frac{1}{4}$ h.). On the other side of the gap traverse into the Aiguillettes couloir. Climb this by steep and quite difficult rocks and ice on its L side (stonefall in bed). Cross a secondary couloir coming down from the L above (from the col behind the Petit Clocher, and before the Clocher) and higher up reach an easement on terraces below the Clocher. Continue up the L side of the couloir towards the col of the Brèche du Clocher (N of the summit) for nearly 100m., then climb steep broken rocks on the R side of the funnel giving access to this col (3805m. VT) (1¾ h.). All the ground from the Brèche du Trident gives sustained climbing at AD/AD+ standard.

Now climb easier rocks diagonally L for 20m. to a steeper wall. Take a jagged crack for 20m. (IV), then hand traverse L for 3m. to where a difficult stride leads to an icy ledge. Follow this to an icy chimney and climb it for 15m. to a ledge on the E ridge close to the summit. Go over large blocks then up a crack (III) to reach the top in 15m. (1 h., 5 h. from Torino hut).

Descent: Either reverse the ascent route to the Brèche du Clocher, or go down 20m. to a ledge and make two abseils of 20m. to another ledge which leads back to this col. From the col abseil down the W couloir to the glacier (stonefall).

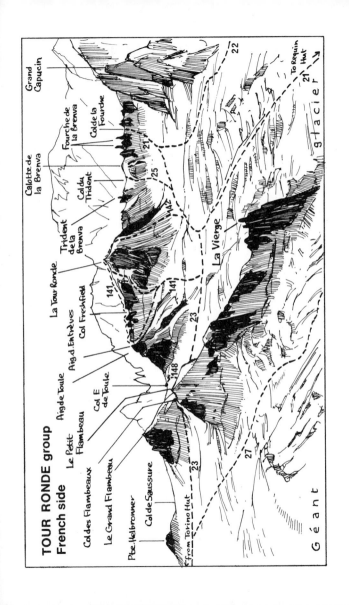

TOUR RONDE group
French side

Grand Capucin

Fourche de la Brenva

Col de la Fourche

Calotte de la Brenva

Col du Trident

Trident de la Brenva

La Tour Ronde

Aig. d. Entrèves

Col Freshfield

Aiguille Toule

Le Petit Flambeau

Col des Flambeaux

Le Grand Flambeau

Pte. Helbronner

Col de Saussure

Col E de Toule

La Vierge

To Requin Hut

glacier

Géant

from Torino Hut

22

21

25

142

141

141

23

148

23

27

21

Tour Ronde - Aiguille de la Brenva group

<u>Frontier Ridge</u>

From the Col de la Fourche (3682m.), at the foot of the Tour Ronde ridge of Mt. Maudit, the frontier ridge continues SE over a series of small pinnacles and cols to the Tour Ronde. The main features are the Fourche bivouac (3680m., Routes 21-24), twin pinnacles of the Fourche de la Brenva (3737, 3730m.), Col de la Calotte (3669m.), Calotte de la Brenva (3701m.), Col du Trident (3679m.), Trident hut (3690m., Routes 25-26), Trident de la Brenva (3720m.) and the double Col de la Tour Ronde (3661m.). From here rises the Tour Ronde (3792m.).

After the Tour Ronde the frontier continues over a series of secondary summits to the Col du Géant. The main features are: Aig. d'Entrèves (3600m.), Col W de Toule (3481m.), Aig. de Toule (3534m.), Col E de Toule (3411m.), Le Grand Flambeau (3559m.) and Pte. Helbronner (3462m.). The Grand Flambeau is an excellent viewpoint and can be reached easily from the Torino hut, either by its N or SE ridges.

The Aig. de la Brenva (3278m.), a major summit in this group, rises on a long spur detached from the frontier ridge just beyond the Tour Ronde.

TOUR RONDE   3792m.

An excellent training peak for climbers based both on the Torino and Requin huts. Very popular with excellent views of the Brenva face and Peuterey ridge. First ascent: J. H. Backhouse, T. H. Carson, D. W. Freshfield and C. C. Tucker with D. Balleys and M. Payot, 22 July, 1867. First winter ascent: Capt. U. Mautino with J. Petigax and C. Croux, c. 1895. First on ski: O. Bérard, A. Bonacossa and B. Salvi Christiani, 12 May, 1917.

<u>South-East Ridge.</u> A pleasant and interesting climb. Direct variations up the face to the R of the ridge are steep, on poor rock and unpleasant. PD. First ascensionists.

141 From the Torino hut cross the Col des Flambeaux and descend a little to the foot of the snow cwm on the E side of the mtn. Go up the middle of this cwm (crevasses) then slant up to the L towards the gap of the Col d'Entrèves. Cross the bergschrund and climb the steep snow slope to the col ($1\frac{1}{2}$ h.). Climb the SE ridge, keeping to the R, then turn a series of gendarmes on the L side. Reach a little snow saddle called Col Freshfield (3625m.) (1 h.) and continue up the easy final slopes to the summit ($3\frac{3}{4}$ h. from Torino hut).

North Face. A short but interesting ice route, giving good practice in snow conditions and technique. Frequently climbed. D-, but the standard varies with conditions. Some stonefall danger in the lower part. Average angle 52°, initial slope, 55°. 330m. First ascent: F. Gonella with A. Berthod, 23 August, 1886. First winter ascent: M. Mai, G. Miglio and E. Russo, 3 February, 1957. First British ascent: I. S. Clough with J. L. Bernezat, 19 June, 1960. Descended on ski by P. Vallençat, 27 June, 1971. First traced solo: A. Socquet, 28 July, 1974.

142 From the Torino hut follow Route 23 to the foot of the N face. Cross the bergschrund towards the R-hand side of the face. It is normally quite difficult. Ascend the steep snow/ice slope above towards the large ice couloir which is the most prominent feature of the face. Either go straight up the couloir or use rocks on its R; the latter is not considered "proper" by purists. At the top of the couloir move L to the foot of the final 30m. tower. Either climb this directly (IV) or, usual, turn it on the L to join the finish of the normal route (4 h. from Torino hut).

143 West (Gervasutti) Couloir. Round the corner from the N face is a large impressive triangular rock facet forming the

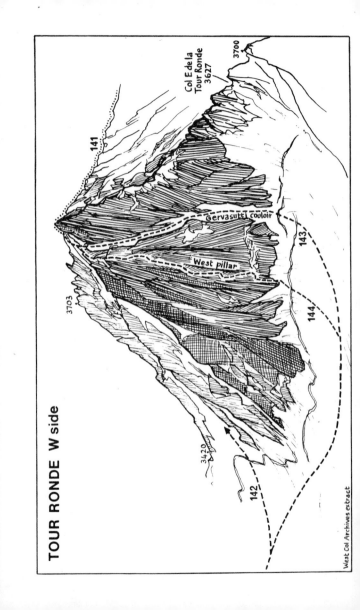

TOUR RONDE W side

141

Col E de la
Tour Ronde
3627

3700

Gervasutti couloir

West pillar

143

144

3703

3420

142

West Col Archives extract

W side of the mtn. Its R side is cut by an ice couloir of about
48° for 250m. An interesting route, not difficult in conditions
of good snow. Keep to the L side for most of the way up. AD.
First ascent: R. Chabod and G. Gervasutti, 27 July, 1934.
Descended on ski in 25 min. by D. Faivre and J. P. Mansart,
31 March, 1974.

<u>West Pillar.</u>   A sustained strenuous climb of easy access
from the Torino hut.   Several pitches of V and V+ with normally 15 pegs and a few wedges in place. 300m. First ascent:
C. Mollier and G. Payot, 23 July, 1961. First winter ascent:
D. Galante, P. Pessa and D. Vota, 4-6 January, 1975.

144 From the Torino hut reach across the Col des Flambeaux
the foot of the N face of the mtn. , then go up into the glacier
bay round the corner, under the W face.   The pillar rises
conspicuously on the L side of the W couloir ($1\frac{1}{2}$ h.). Cross a
sometimes difficult bergschrund and climb the R side of the
lowest rocks by a chimney (25m. , IV+) till a traverse R leads
to a ledge. Traverse R along a flake for 10m. (IV+, V+) to a
narrow crack and go up this (V) till a step L to a slab is
followed by a pull up on to a sloping ledge (40m., V+). Above,
continue up a flake which leads to a dièdre (V), then climb
flakes for 35m. (IV+) to the top of the first section of the
pillar.

Descend L into a gap and climb an icy couloir/chimney.
Then traverse R and climb a crack on the R of a slab (40m. ,
IV, V). Continue up a slanting crack (IV+) and follow the continuation crack (40m. , V, V+). Another dièdre/crack above
is taken (V, V+) till it overhangs. Now go L and by a flake
pull up on to a slab which is climbed to the foot of a dièdre
(40m. , V, V+). Take the dièdre a short way then trend R on
flakes to another dièdre. Climb this (V, IV+) and exit R by a
crack in a slab (IV+). Traverse R along a large flake (IV+) to

reach a snow rib and follow this to a pitch up to the R, taken by a flake then a slab and a couloir/chimney (V, IV). Above this a dièdre to the L then a slab to the R (40m., IV, V, A1). Belay in the middle of the slab. Above, climb L round a gendarme and reach the NW ridge just below the exit of the W couloir.

Follow the ridge and traverse L (N) above the N face and under the summit tower to rejoin the normal route (6-7 h. from bergschrund).

South Face. A useful descent (or ascent) via the Brenva bivouac to Courmayeur. PD.

145 From the summit descend a short way along the SW ridge then strike off down the S face, first by a rib of snowy rocks then by a steep snow slope. This leads over a bergschrund into the upper basin of the E branch of the Brenva glacier (2 h.). Descend the glacier to a crevassed zone, then traverse R on to the rognon on which the Brenva bivouac is situated (30 min., $2\frac{1}{2}$ h. from summit, $3\frac{1}{2}$ h. in ascent).

TÊTE DE LA BRENVA   3504m.

A rock tower to the SE of the Tour Ronde, at the head of the ridge leading down to the Aig. de la Brenva. First ascent: A. Hess and H. Martiny with L. Mussillon, 24 August, 1902.

South-West Face. A fine rock climb of 500m. with pitches of IV and V. First ascent: P. Ghiglione and A. Ottoz, 24 July, 1948.

146 From the Brenva bivouac descend into the upper basin of the E branch of the Brenva glacier and traverse the glacier descending slightly to the foot of the SW face of the Tête de la Brenva ($1\frac{1}{2}$ h.).

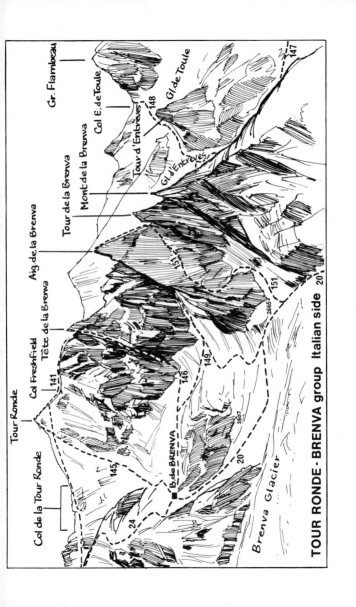

TOUR RONDE - BRENVA group Italian side

The centre of the face is split by a long narrow couloir. Cross the bergschrund L of the couloir and climb smooth rocks (IV) to a broken ledge. Traverse the ledge diagonally R then climb broken rocks to reach the couloir about 150m. above the bergschrund. Cross the couloir to a vertical chimney and climb this for 20m. (IV and V). Traverse R and climb a second chimney, sometimes iced up, and continue to a small gap. Descend several m. on to the S face, follow a ledge and climb to another gap. Traverse towards the SE, rising slightly, and climb a smooth chimney (IV), then an overhang (V) to reach a gap with a small gendarme. Descend several m. on slabs, make a long stride into a diagonal crack and climb it for 5m. (V). Traverse slabs and climb a chimney, trending towards the W, to reach a secondary summit then the top ($4\frac{1}{2}$ h., 6 h. from Brenva bivouac).

In descent follow the short NW ridge to a small col then climb up to the Col d'Entrèves. Then continue by Route 141 to the Torino hut; or traverse the Tour Ronde and descend by Route 145 to the Brenva bivouac.

BRÈCHE DE LA BRENVA   3135m.

Between the Tête de la Brenva and the Aig. de la Brenva. A fairly easy col affording a convenient passage from the Entrèves glacier to the Brenva glacier. Some stonefall danger on the Entrèves side. First traverse: E. H. F. Bradby, J. H. Wicks and C. Wilson, 25 July, 1904.

147 From Courmayeur take the cableway to the Pavillon. From here follow the well marked track going up to the Torino hut for about 30 min., then make a long slightly rising traverse across the grassy hillside, well below the level of the Toule glacier (traces of path). Cross several glacier streams and moraines and reach the moraine at the foot of the Entrèves glacier, just at the foot of the S ridge of the Aig. d'Entrèves, at c. 2580m. Climb the Entrèves glacier to the foot of the couloir leading to the Brèche de la Brenva. Cross the bergschrund and climb straight up the couloir to the col. PD (3 h. from Pavillon).

The couloir leading to the col is subject to stonefall and the following climbing variation is safer.

Start up the rocks R of the couloir in a line directly below a small gap in the ridge above. Climb a well marked dièdre obvious from above the bergschrund (50m., IV, V). Continue up the dièdre for another 50m. (IV+, IV, III) until it is possible to break out L on short walls and slabs. The angle eases, go diagonally L towards a rib of poor rock which is followed to the col (M. Burke, B. Clarke, J. S. Cleare and M. Kosterlitz, August, 1967).

148 From the Torino hut follow Route 23 across the Col des Flambeaux and contour round the base of the Grand Flambeau to reach the Col E de Toule (3411m.), overlooking the Toule glacier. Descend the short steep couloir on to the glacier, trending to the R, and descend the glacier trending well over to the R to reach the Brèche d'Entrèves (3070m. IGM). This col is not marked on IGN. It is situated in the ridge NW of the Tour d'Entrèves (3124m.). The lower (SE) of two gaps is the proper crossing place. Cross the col and descend a steep couloir on to the Entrèves glacier. Rise slightly across the glacier to join Route 147 at the foot of the couloir leading up to the col (2 h.). In good snow conditions this is a quick and convenient route and is recommended as an approach to climbs on the E face of the Aig. de la Brenva. PD/PD+.

149 From the Brenva bivouac descend into the upper basin of the E branch of the Brenva glacier. Traverse the glacier, under the S face of the Tête de la Brenva, to the tiny glacier leading up to the col. Avoid crevasses by keeping to the L side and climb a short couloir to the col. PD ($2\frac{1}{2}$ h.).

LE PÈRE ETERNAL 3224m.

A fantastic pinnacle about 60m. high on its long side, between the Aig. de la Brenva and Brèche de la Brenva. The ascent of the pinnacle can be conveniently combined with that of the N ridge of the Aig. de la Brenva, but in fact neither has been climbed often.

<u>North-West Ridge.</u> A short delicate climb, mainly V and V+. First ascent: L. Grivel, A. and O. Ottoz and A. Pennard, 7 August, 1927.

150 From the Brèche de la Brenva climb snowy rocks to the foot of the pinnacle. Climb a short ice couloir on the L to a small col between the pinnacle and a small gendarme to its N. Cross the col and traverse across a slab to a crack which leads up to the Brèche du Père Eternal, between the pinnacle and the Aig. de la Brenva. Traverse the Brenva side of the pinnacle along an easy ascending ledge. Climb a delicate wall (V) to a small sloping platform on the NW ridge. Climb a fixed ladder for 5m. then the steep wall on the L (V) to an overhang. Avoid the overhang on the R (peg) and continue up to a second overhang (3 pegs) which is avoided by a hand traverse to the L. Continue straight up the ridge to the top (1-2 h.). In descent, two abseils to the easy ascending ledge near the Brèche du Père Eternal.

AIGUILLE DE LA BRENVA 3278m. 3269m. IGN

An interesting peak with a fine E face. As a training exercise it is a stiff walk from Courmayeur but done quite often. First ascent: A. Hess with L. Croux and C. Ollier, 25 August, 1898.

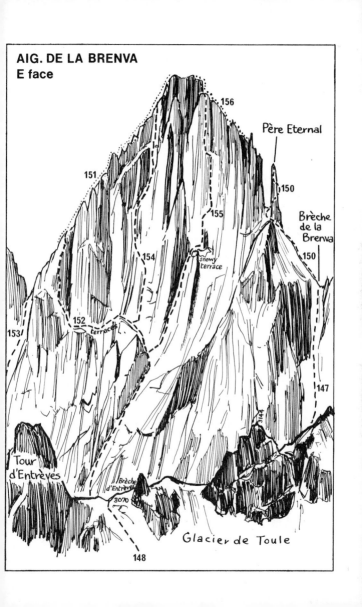

AIG. DE LA BRENVA
E face

<u>South-East Ridge (Normal Route)</u>. An interesting and frequently ascended climb. PD. First ascensionists.

151 From Courmayeur/Entrèves follow Route 20 to the foot of the SW ridge (2665m.) of the mtn. (4 h.). Climb R into a snowy cwm below the S face, and soon work round to the L to climb an easy chimney to the R-hand end of a grassy terrace on the lower part of the SW ridge. Continue up a couloir to the crest of this ridge, and follow it easily to a pointed gendarme above the R side of the couloir. From here traverse across the S face of the mtn. on easy rocks and ledges to reach the large col at the foot of the SE ridge, between the Aig. and Tour de la Brenva ($1\frac{1}{2}$ h.).

Continue up the SE ridge avoiding difficulties by keeping L all the way. Near the summit make a traverse L across a slab then climb straight up to the serrated summit ridge. Cross the subsidiary towers to the third one, which is the highest pt. ($1\frac{1}{2}$ h., 7 h. from Courmayeur).

<u>East Face and South-East Ridge</u>. The easiest and least direct of the routes on the E face. Continuously interesting climbing mainly with pitches of IV and bits of IV+. First ascent: Nina Pietrasanta and G. Boccalatte, 16 August, 1934.

152 From the Pavillon or Torino hut follow Routes 147 or 148 to the foot of the E face of the mtn. Start from the highest pt. of the snowfield under the face, directly below an obvious gully system higher up the face. Cross the bergschrund, sometimes difficult, and climb a steep crack (IV, pegs) to a platform. Continue up to the R in a chimney/couloir for 30m. to a chockstone. Climb this (III+) and move R into a larger couloir. Follow its R side easily for 60m. until it steepens. Climb a short smooth chimney (IV+) to where the couloir is blocked above. Move L into a shallow groove (IV) L of the main gully line, then go up a steep wall on the R (IV+, peg) to easier ground and a cave belay. Climb the chimney L out of the cave and continue up chimney/cracks (III+) to a final short vertical chimney leading to the lowest ledge of a terrace system, half-way up this L side of the E face ($1\frac{1}{2}$ - 2 h.).

Traverse L along the terraces, descending slightly, to the couloir which descends from the large groove on the L of the E face. Cross the couloir and climb to a broken ledge. Cross the ledge and climb small couloirs and chimneys to the SE ridge. Follow this (Route 151) to the summit ($2\frac{1}{2}$-3 h., 4-5 h. from foot of face).

<u>Descent to the Entrèves glacier.</u> A convenient descent for returning via the Pavillon. G. Moro, A. and T. Romanengo with O. Bron and L. Proment, 20 August, 1926.

153 Descend the SE ridge (Route 151) to the large gap between the Aig. and Tour de la Brenva. Descend the couloir on the Entrèves side for 50m., then make a descending traverse R across the E face of the Tour, on steep but easy rocks, until above a steep smooth wall. Abseil 25m. down this wall, then down a steep groove to a shoulder. Pegs in place. Now descend to the L for 30m. then traverse L into a couloir running down to the glacier. Climb or abseil down this to reach the glacier about 75m. from the starting pt. of the E face routes. Continue by Route 147 to the Pavillon (2-3 h.).

<u>East Face (Via Boccalatte).</u> A bold climb with continuous difficulties in the upper part. Some doubtful rock on the hardest pitches. V/V+, pegs normally in place. 350m. First ascent: Nina Pietrasanta and G. Boccalatte, 12 July, 1935. First British ascent: M. J. Harris and J. Neill, 1954.

154 Follow Route 152 to the terraces halfway up the L side of the E face. Just below the highest ledge, move R across a smooth overlapped slab (V) into an obvious crack line which goes directly towards the summit. Climb this for 15m. (IV) to a small stance and peg belay. Continue steeply up the crack for 30m. (V+, pegs) to another small stance. Now climb to the R for 6m. to a small ledge, then traverse horizontally L across a vertical yellow wall (V+) to a yellow block. Climb the steep crack above (V+, pegs) to the foot of a shallow couloir. Climb this for 25m. then move L to a ridge (IV, peg). Continue up the ridge then easier broken ground to join the SE ridge about 50m. from the summit (4-6 h. from foot of face).

East Face (Rébuffat Route). An excellent free climb using a later variation finish, described below, which is more direct than the original finish. The latter involved a rope traverse and pitches of VI-/A1. About the same standard as the Via Boccalatte and perhaps finer. V/V+, 390m. First ascent: J. Deudon and B. Pierre with G. Rébuffat, 18-19 May, 1948. First winter ascent: P. Gleize and J. Keller, March, 1975.

155 Follow Route 152 to just below the short vertical chimney giving access to the terraces halfway up the E face. Move R to a ledge and traverse diagonally across a wall (IV) into the obvious groove which descends from the summit ridge, marking the general line of the lower part of the route. Climb the groove (III and IV) then stride L and take an overhanging crack to the L (V+, pegs). Continue up the groove until it widens into a chimney (IV+). Break out on to the face on the R and climb a series of chimneys and ascending ledges to a large terrace, normally snow covered. Continue straight up for 15m. (IV+), traverse 10m. R, then climb returning gradually L on poor rock (IV+ with moves of V). Continue for a few m. then traverse L to the foot of an obvious dièdre (V/V+, pegs). At this pt. the original finish traversed R to a dièdre line running up to the summit.

Climb the dièdre above to a ledge and blocks (IV+). Take

212

the chimney above (IV), followed by a flake pitch (III) then a slab (V) ending in an overhang. Turn the overhang on the R (V) and enter a chimney. Climb this to the summit (IV then III) (5-6 h. from foot of face).

<u>North Ridge.</u> An interesting climb of 150m., rarely done. Pitches of V/V+, strenuous. First ascent: Signorina S. Olivetti with O. Ottoz and F. Thomasset, 31 July, 1933.

156 From the Brèche de la Brenva follow Route 150 to the Brèche du Père Eternal. Traverse round the E flank of a small gendarme to reach the foot of the first step. Climb the Brenva side up a cracked wall (peg) and make an ascending traverse to the R (V, pegs). Follow cracked walls to reach the gap between the first and second steps. Climb short steep walls for 10m. to the foot of a steep crack (V, pegs). Follow this diagonally R for 30m. to an exposed niche (V+, pegs, 6 wedges, very strenuous). Climb a slightly overhanging groove (V+, pegs) to a ledge. Climb a small bulge then a wall on the E side to the top of the second step. Follow the crest of the ridge with a short section of V to the summit (2-3 h. from Brèche de la Brenva).

COL DU GÉANT 3365m. 3354m. IGM 3359m. VT

Between Pte. Helbronner and the Aigs. Marbrées. One of the most famous glacier passes in the Alps, crossing the Mt. Blanc range at its midway pt. and linking Chamonix and Courmayeur. Both sides on foot are easy; but the French side is long, and complicated by the Géant icefall above the Requin hut. See Routes 27, 28, 29. Nowadays the communication can be made using either the Midi cableway or the Mt. Blanc road tunnel.
    First traverse: J. M. Cachet and A. Tournier, 27 June, 1787. First winter traverse: C. D. Cunningham and three guides, 27 January, 1882.

INDEX OF ROUTES SHOWN ON DIAGRAMS

Route number	Diagram on page(s)
39	58,60
40	58,60
41	60
42	64
43	64
44	64
45	64
46	60
47	60
48	88
49	74,88
50	74
51	74
52	72
53	72,82,88
54	72
55	72
56	72,82
57	88
58	88
59	88
60	82,86,96
61	82,86
62	82,86
63	86,96
64	96
65	96
66	96
67	96
68	96
69	96
70	96

General Index